Swinging from A to Z

By Larry Fine and Mia Fine

Copyright © 2010 Larry Fine and Mia Fine

All rights reserved. No part of this book may be used or reproduced in any manner whatsoever without prior written permission from the publisher except in the case of brief quotations used in critical articles and reviews.

First edition: Published April 2010

Allure Publishing
Allure.Publishing@yahoo.com

Printed in the United States of America.

Swinging from A to Z

A how-to guide from a full-swap Lifestyle couple
for enhancing your relationship with recreational sex

By Larry Fine and Mia Fine

Allure Publishing

April 2010

L & M are as real as it gets. He is very engaging and absolutely hilarious, while she is beautiful, sexy, and incredible fun to be with. *(Blkezrider, Tampa, Fla.)*

Both of them not only define the word HOT but even contribute to Global Warming to a big extent. Great attitude, perfect conversationalists, and fun to be around. Lifestyle-wise, they are a drama free, passionate full-swap couple who know how to make your head spin. *(Ilkoety, Harriman, N.Y.)*

Charming and engaging, L & M had my attention at first sight. She is an exquisite, sensual beauty and he is her handsome, strong, yet gentle counterpart. They were sophisticated, warm, and welcoming, and sweet with a smile here, a nod of encouragement there, yet never pushy, which added to the aura of subtle seduction. *(Marissa, Fort Lee, N.J.)*

A classy, fun-loving and erotic couple who complement each other. He is cool and laid back. She is sexy and vivacious. *(Hedo89, Monroe, N.Y.)*

...intimate erotic moments with these two are real, no faking, no BS; truly from the depth of passion and compassion. He is the sweetest and one of the most responsive and intense lovers. She is a dream: soft, flowing, sweet, and seductive with the most sensual voice. Meet them, open your mind, and experience a new path to erotic fulfillment, beyond any shallow description. *(Tommy & Jessica, Kansas City, Mo.)*

...they are as good as it gets in the Lifestyle. *(Steven & Liz, Princeton, N.J.)*

Warning: addictive couple! You'll ask for more and more. *(Brazilianflavor, New York, N.Y.)*

L & M exemplify everything that a perfect couple in the Lifestyle should...class, fun, sensuality, humor, intelligence, zero-drama...and she always is dressed in something HOT! *(Mark & Dee, Syracuse, N.Y.)*

L & M are the whole package! Very sexy, interesting, intelligent, wild and certainly know how to host a party. *(Beth & Larry, Nyack, N.Y.)*

WOW! The definition of class, sexuality, fun, and let us not forget TALENT. We met these two at Entice convention and had lots of fun.... Don't miss an opportunity to be with these two, whether it's a night of dancing and laughs, or, if you are lucky, much, much more. *(Angie & Christian, Boston, Mass.)*

She is as sexy on the dance floor as she is off. They both do everything with finesse and flourish. He is quite the charmer/seducer and has bragging rights to being a good lover and keeping up the steady pace. They are both animated in their endeavors and are smoking! Sizzzz *(Jezebel, Toronto, Canada)*

...they are all that and a box of cherries on top! They are what their profile states and we can attest to their sweet, sensual, and classy nature. They are fabulous in and out of bed. We truly enjoyed our memory-making encounter with two true swingers! *(Soundman, Southern Oregon)*

They are truly a fun duo, who care about each other, and really enjoy the Lifestyle for all the good things it has to offer. ...They are the most genuine couple you would ever want to meet. *(Jaybry6, Sparta, N.J.)*

Foreword

> *If we do not find anything pleasant,*
> *at least we shall find something new.*
> —*Voltaire*

We wrote this book for want-to-be-swingers and beginners. But many seasoned swingers also will find helpful tips here to boost their experience in the Lifestyle.

This book is *subjective*, so it's not a scientific study of the Lifestyle. We just wanted to share regular people's irregular experiences and our suggestions for helping you enter and enjoy the swinging Lifestyle.

The primary targets of the book are couples, whether married or not. Swinging is all about couples.

A lot of swinging singles of both sexes add to the fun, and we promise to discuss them as well, but we'll do it from the couple's perspective.

We are a married couple. We *share* the beliefs we espouse here, as well as the swinging experience between us, equally.

We wrote some chapters of this book separately; others we wrote jointly and bylined them as such.

If you have a particular interest in something we might have missed, or if you just need a direct answer to a simple question, please e-mail us at allure.publishing@yahoo.com. We promise to respond to your queries if they aren't personal. The most interesting questions and our answers could become a solid base for the second edition of this book.

To protect individual privacy, we changed the names, nicknames, website profile handles, etc. we referred to (including our own). The people mentioned are real people. All their stories and experiences are true. But swingers are as discreet as possible to avoid fallout from anyone who would criticize their life choices.

—Larry and Mia Fine

Dedication

To my beloved wife:

Darling,
You have made my life a true delight. I am the happiest person in the whole universe!

To my dearest husband:

Honey,
Because of you, I feel myself a Woman! You walk me through the best times I ever could dream of. I truly appreciate your trust and love you like never before!

Contents

Foreword 7

Dedication 8

Chapter 1: Getting started in the Lifestyle

The Lifestyle may become your choice! 13
The modern meaning of an old word 14
Some terminology 15
Why swinging? 16
Swinging might be your sexual revolution 19
The golden rule of swinging 20
Varieties of swing 21
Something else to consider 25
Swinging is addictive 26
How much does swinging cost? 27

Chapter 2: Marriage and swinging

Is swinging moral enough? 31
How to make that tough decision 32
What are the initial options? 36
The Lifestyle is all about sharing 40
Proper safety measures 41

Chapter 3: Dating couples

Couple is the core Lifestyle measurement unit 45
Doing one for the team 47

Setting the rules 50
First dates 51
Swinging and friendship 56
Friendship and swinging 61
Full swap or soft swap? 63
Same room or separate rooms? 64
Tweaking the age 67
Women rule the Lifestyle 68

Chapter 4: The Lifestyle vs. vanilla

Who are those swingers anyway? 71
Are you attractive? 73
Confidence, attitude, and chemistry are the keys 75
Are swingers aggressive? 76
Age and swing 77
What do swingers talk about? 79
Swinging is a show! 82

Chapter 5: Meeting on Internet

Swing websites 87
Your profile on a swing website 88
Communicating on the Web 99
Fakes and flakes 101
How to spot a weird profile 102

Chapter 6: Meeting others in person

Your Lifestyle business card 105
Meet-and-Greets 106
Swing clubs 108
Off-premise clubs 109
On-premise clubs 112
Club strategies 114
Swinging and jealousy 117
If it doesn't want to get up 119
Private parties 121
Commercial swing parties 123
Non-commercial parties 124
If you are ever up to host your own parties 126
Optimal M/F balance at parties 133
Single males and single females in the Lifestyle 135

Chapter 7: Swing resorts and conventions

Hedo mania 143
Hedo vs. Desire 150
Swing conventions 152
Approaching at resorts and conventions 154

Chapter 8: Your look

What to wear in the Lifestyle 159
Your attire at a theme party 162
Your clothes at resorts 165

Chapter 9: Sex

Group play and orgies 169
Bisexuality and the Lifestyle 173
Does size matter? 176
Interracial sexual contacts 179
Get in the right mood! 182

Glossary

Common Lifestyle terms and abbreviations 185

Index 189

Chapter 1

Getting Started in the Lifestyle

The Lifestyle may become your choice
By Larry and Mia

> Sex is one of the nine reasons for reincarnation.
> The other eight are unimportant.
> —Henry Miller

> I remember, as a kid going to Hebrew school, how disappointed I was when I found out that Adam was a schmuck. God gave him a woman and an apple—and he ate the apple!
> —Norm Crosby

Be honest with yourself to answer these questions:
- Would you be interested in having sex with someone twice your age or someone twice as young?
- Would you enjoy a threesome?
- Would you benefit from a sexual encounter with five partners at the same time or one after another?
- Would you be willing to participate in some kind of wild orgy with 30 to 40 naked people in one room?

Add one point for each *positive* answer.

Next group of questions (remember, honesty is the key):
- Are you happy with the sexual part of your life?
- Do you think your life partner is completely sexually satisfied (even if you are)?

- Have you fulfilled all your sexual fantasies?
- Have you completely explored your sexuality?

Add one point for each *negative* response.

If your total score is zero, you likely don't have an interest in the swing Lifestyle. Please accept our deepest thanks for participating in the test. If your score is between one and eight, you may pick up something helpful from this book.

We hope our book lights the way for people to enhance their relationship with their significant others and bring it to the point where they can *together* answer "yes" to these questions—"together" being the key word.

Frankly, if you picked up this book, its subject makes you at least curious, and this fact alone means the Lifestyle may become your choice.

The modern meaning of an old word

By Larry

A little history tour...

The word "swing" comes from the 1920s when jazz was born. Its second name, swinging jazz, is where this word takes its roots from: the new form of dance linked to it.

In the 1930s and 1940s, the big band era, swinging music grew in popularity and "Swing was king."

By the 1950s, though, new singing stars, such as Belafonte, Martin, Cole, Primo, and, of course, Sinatra, reinvented the word "swinger" and gave it a new life. This word started to represent their lifestyle rather than ordinary music associations. These guys were passionate and fashionable, cool and perfect. They were *swingers*. *Playboy* magazine started in those days and sexuality as a basic human function turned into an object of wide public curiosity. The word "swinger" had received a positive subtext, and everyone wanted to be one.

The *Shagedelic* 1960s followed, and the term "swinging" was first associated with certain sexual activities. Swing clubs as well as alternative relationships (swinging, communal living, and polyamory) started to form toward the end of the 1960s.

The 1970s introduced new sexual innovations, such as *wife swappers* and *key parties*. Wife swappers became *new swingers* and the swinging Lifestyle was born.

Nowadays, the swinging Lifestyle is an industry and a powerful economic factor. Swing clubs have popped up in every large city. Swing conventions with thousands of attendees are common. Books and articles in prestigious magazines, as well as shows on popular cable networks, resorts, hotels, and even cruise ships cater to swingers like never before.

Some terminology
By Larry and Mia

Would you like vanilla?

Swingers are people who participate in recreational open sex activities. *The Lifestyle* is just another term for swinging. For instance, instead of asking, "Are you a swinger?" you could ask, "Are you in the Lifestyle?"

Swingers commonly use the word "Lifestyle" with the capital "L." They refer to other swinging people as "gentlemen" and "ladies."

The antonym to swing is *vanilla,* which is everything and everyone outside the swinging world. "I had to attend that boring vanilla party instead of having real fun." You can hear something like that often enough at swingers' get-togethers.

The word "friend" has likewise transformed. If you hear "friend" from swingers, they mean their Lifestyle friends or else they would say "vanilla friend." They may also refer to "horizontal friends" and "vertical friends," respectively.

Swingers often use the F-word. We have never met anyone in the Lifestyle offended by this practice. Still, the Lifestylers use the word "play" more often since it characterizes swinging activities more precisely showing we swingers aren't too serious with what we do. Swinging is just fun, just play.

Why swinging?
By *Larry and Mia*

> There are good marriages, but no delightful ones.
> —*La Rochefoucauld*

> "Sex" is as important as eating or drinking and we ought to allow the one appetite to be satisfied with as little restraint or false modesty as the other.
> —*Marquis de Sade*

If you wish your lover to cheat on you, marry him.

We need food to eat, water to drink, air to breathe. No one would argue with that.

Furthermore, we all have several necessities built into our bodies and pre-set into our minds. Having sex is one of them. Besides the pure, natural need for sex, we are carrying sexual feelings, fantasies, and desires with us throughout most of our lives.

Sex plays an enormous role in human life. According to researchers of the Kinsey Institute for Research in Sex, Gender, and Reproduction at Indiana University, men are always thinking about sex. By that, they mean 54% of men think about sex several times a day, compared with just 19% of women.

Do you think that's a lot? It's nothing if neuropsychiatrist Dr. Louann Brizendine, author of *The Female Brain*, is correct. She writes in her book that men think about sex every 52 seconds, while women tend to think of it just once a day.

No matter how often we think of sex (and how strongly we might be preoccupied with sexual desires), the reality is clear: sex is a basic human instinct that significantly controls our minds. It is a reason for many of our thoughts and actions. Many historical examples prove that sex greatly affects our behavior. We don't have to go deep in the past. Recent scandals involving A-list celebrities as well as first-grade politicians (do you recall that smooth transition of 'The Oval Office' into 'The Oral Office'?) should be more than enough to prove the above statement.

As swingers, the authors never equate love and sex. No swingers do. Love is an individual feeling and translates differently for every one of us. We might just live for our loved one, and we cannot imagine our existence without him or her.

Sex is different. We can have it with anyone with just one condition—we should have sexual desire for our prospective playmate. Besides being mostly physiological, plain sex is emotional and pleasurable by itself. However, these emotions have nothing to do with our sex partner *as a person*.

If you disagree with that premise, perhaps you've never had sex just for the sake of it. Caring about your sex partner is wonderful if he/she is the love of your life. If you have any likewise personal feelings for your playmate while having sex outside your relationship, you are in trouble. Something is likely wrong with you or your relationship (or both).

Mother Nature has programmed humans to be *polygamists*. Doubtful? Have you ever cheated on a loved one? Would you go for it if you knew for sure nobody would ever learn? Have you never even thought about having sex with someone other than your significant other?

After being together for a considerable time (for some of us it can take two or three years, for some 20 or 30 years), we start to feel something is missing from our used-to-be-perfect relationship. We could love each other more than ever, we could have beautiful children, own big houses and expensive cars, be successful at business, and yet feel something is wrong. Our sexual interactions become once-a-week, routine, fully predictable, and not exciting events. Time flies, and sexuality slowly dies while unsatisfied sexual fantasies grow.

Some of us just live with it. Some start looking for satisfaction outside a relationship by cheating on our partners. Neither helps the relationship, but feeling and acting that way is natural and normal. Mother Nature made us this way.

Dear Cheaters, ask yourselves, "Is it necessary to risk everything you've built in your life for those moments of sexual excitement and a few orgasms? What is more important: the love of your life and happiness of your family...or sex on the side?" We anticipate your answer being something like, "Yes, I know, but I am unable to stop. It happens by itself."

Similar to having the same dish for every dinner, listening to the same music every night, watching the same show every weekend (even if that is your favorite dish, music, and show respectively), having sex with only one partner doesn't work well for most of us in the long run. It becomes less satisfying and boring in the end.

What is the solution? Should we divorce and then re-marry? It won't help much. We will end up in the same situation; this time even faster than before.

Could cheating help? Only if we like to live in the chaos of arrangements being kept in deep secret from everyone. Only if we are ready to erase dialed and received numbers from our phone, to face the hell of permanent dishonesty with our life partners, and, finally, the real possibility of a divorce.

However, letting sexuality die isn't a viable option for most.

Some couples try to resolve their internal sex-related issues by turning to prostitutes, one of them, or even both. Others end up with open relationships. They agree to meet other people for having sex separately from each other.

This solution could work for a small group of people but would require a lot of trust on both sides. It could satisfy their sexual desires on a certain level. If they were lucky enough to control themselves fully, this arrangement wouldn't damage their relationship. Although, it wouldn't bring it to the new and better stage since life partners aren't going through fun times together. What's more, they might break the hearts of people they play with. Due to those people's *vanilla* mindset, many of them would expect you to leave your loved ones for them.

The real answer is simple and depends on us and only on us. If we truly intend to keep our relationship on solid ground and at the same time enhance its sexual part, if we are interested in sincerity between us, if we want to explore our sexuality, open new, unfamiliar sexual sides of each other, and make it happen together, swinging answers all our problems.

Swinging might be your sexual revolution
By Larry and Mia

> *Part of the sexual revolution is bringing rationality to sexuality—because when you don't embrace sexuality in a normal way, you get the twisted kinds, and the kinds that destroy lives.*
> —Hugh Hefner

Play together to stay together!

Swinging is not for everyone. We know several couples who have tried swinging but stopped. We also know couples who are in the process of finding their swinging ways for several years and still are in the same spot in that process. Some of our friends took years to get into the Lifestyle fully, while others got there quickly and easily. The authors happily belong to the last group.

Swinging is not a universal one-for-all prescription, not a perfect cure. It won't heal a broken relationship. Instead, it may destroy what is left of it.

At the same time, joining the Lifestyle while your relationship is strong and based on a two-way trust opens for both of you a highest level of sensuality. It leads to real sexual satisfaction and, therefore, brings the relationship itself to the new stage where you totally trust each other and love each other more passionately than you ever did before. Besides, being in the Lifestyle is just incredible fun that you never suspected you could have.

The golden rule of swinging
By Larry

Sex is not the answer. Sex is the question. "Yes" is the answer.
—*Swami X*

Having sex is a mutual agreement.

For the beginners: perhaps many of your discomforts and concerns would go away if you knew the Lifestyle has *the Rule* (yes, with a capital "R").

"No means no"—nobody in the Lifestyle will force you to do anything you don't want to do.

When you become an experienced swinger, you won't need this rule anymore. A real swinger would never play with a partner who doesn't enjoy playing with him or her. If it's not fun, what's the point?

At the club or at the house party, though, swingers will ask you to play with them. However, if you decline once, they will never insist but will simply move on. They understand and hold no hard feelings. Moreover, if someone is too pushy, it only means he is not a real swinger and, therefore, the party hosts or security personnel will ask him to leave and will never welcome him back.

To decline, you are free to use anything from a simple "Thanks, not interested" to just moving your shoulder away, letting the person know you do not accept his or her touch. These methods all work well.

Many related rules exist, such as rules of parties' hosts, swing club owners, etc. For instance, "No cameras and cell phones," "No food and drinks at playroom," "No closed doors." Swing clubs or party hosts will always familiarize you with their internal rules one way or another. They will write them at the reception area or include into your party invitation, and so on.

Although, the main Rule may or may not be explicitly written at the given club or invitation, you can be 100% sure everyone in the Lifestyle supports it. Swinging couldn't exist without it!

Varieties of swing
By Larry

Sex is a body-contact sport. It is safe to watch, but more fun to play.
—Thomas S. Szasz

What's on the menu?

Realize that swinging is always what you want it to be (with the permission of the fellow playmates). Do whatever is best for you, whatever gives you and your loved one maximum pleasure and satisfaction, and whatever brings you the most fun.

Within a reasonable time (again, reasonable for both of you), you will find your place in the Lifestyle world. Don't be afraid to experiment and open new horizons.

Everything that leads to your pleasure is valid as long as it feels good. Remember, swinging should be fun. If it is not, you are doing something wrong. The beauty of the Lifestyle is that you do not need anyone's approval, and, whatever you are interested in, you are likely to find it.

The Lifestyle accommodates many activities. The following are the most common ones listed in order from minimum to maximum physical involvement.

Voyeurism

"Voyeurism" is watching others while they are having sex. Some people prefer watching others at clubs and swing parties. Some don't even take their clothes off.

If you happen to fall within the voyeur category, it's fine if you keep your distance from couples whose activities you are watching. If you intend to get closer, though, remember that not everyone likes to perform for others and can easily label you as freaks, which will make people avoid you.

To make sure you don't annoy anyone, always ask people whose activities you intend to watch if they are okay with it. Remember, even if you are not physically involved with them, you are still trying to participate. If you are watching swingers secretly, you are stealing. If they accept you as voyeurs, you are swinging.

You could use voyeurism as your first step in swinging. Visit an on-premise swing club, watch, and have mind-blowing sex with each other at home afterward. Just make sure you do not stay long at this stage. Frankly, other swingers would not take you seriously if you do. Among our friends, we label curious watchers as "dancers." They never proceed further than dirty dancing and watching others.

Exhibitionism

Exhibitionism in the Lifestyle has a slightly different definition compared to the common one. It is not a "psychological disorder causing a compulsion to show the genitals in public." A couple would be exhibitionists in the Lifestyle terms if they seek satisfaction from having sex with each other while being watched. Swinging is what the swingers want it to be and, therefore, you'll find no perverts in the Lifestyle.

True exhibitionists do not seek a partner exchange. They are a kind of sexual performers for others.

One of our first swinging experiences was sex with exhibitionists. We met Vic and Marsha at Hedonism II in Jamaica and often spotted them having sex with each other in public. They told us they have no interest in anything but exposing their intimacy.

Since we were newbies at the time and wanted to explore a little of everything, we invited them to our room to have some fun together. They agreed on one condition—we had to play by their rules. The rules were easy enough: no physical contact with them besides light touches. Two couples simply had sex in the same bed watching each other. Frankly, even then we were only somewhat satisfied in the end. As we later came to understand, we needed more than that.

Soft swap

This activity would be right for you if in your play you intend to do anything up to but not sexual intercourse with other couples or singles. Yes, you exchange (swap) partners, but only up to a certain extent. Many start with being "softies." Others stay at this stage for many years. Again, it is up to you.

Full swap

Opposite of the above, full swap suggests unconditional partner exchange. If you are full-swappers, you are interested in sexual intercourse.

Threesomes

Threesomes are often what some couples only shoot for. A couple invites either a single gentleman or a single lady to join them. They are happy enough adding just one partner to their sexual activities and are not interested in adding two or more.

At times, only half a couple actually plays at threesomes. The other half prefers to watch his/her partner in action. Many of our friends are couples where the husbands enjoy watching their wives. Moreover, some wives like to watch their husbands' orgasm from a distance, too. Nonetheless, these are still threesomes since both partners participate in the action.

Physical contact is not the only parameter that defines swinging. A combination of physical and emotional factors does. Therefore, you two are only able to mix that perfect cocktail having the most delicious proportion of right ingredients in it.

Foursomes and moresomes

If you add two or more single males or females (or both) to your party, sexual activity can be qualified as foursome or moresome. You two as a couple are still the main link, component, and ruling element of this kind of activity. Some use the term "foursome" to define two couples' play. We prefer the term "couple-to-couple play."

Couple-to-couple play

Being the most popular activity in the Lifestyle, couple-to-couple play is the most complicated one. For both these reasons, the authors will present details on this subject separately. *(See Chapter 3: Dating Couples.)*

Group sex

Group sex is a swinging activity involving more than two couples (plus singles if you wish them to join your fun) playing in one room while doing virtually anything that is suitable and fun for them. Many people initiate group play at swing clubs and private swing parties.

Gangbangs

One, two, or more couples invite several single gentlemen to make their ladies happy. The authors used to host gangbangs with three to four couples and up to 12 guys. They were a great experience. As expected, all our ladies were satisfied like never before. Of course, husbands in such situations have to be prepared to take it a little slower than usual. Waiting lines are long!

Orgies

Some use this term for group sex described above. We would rather separate the two. In our experience, and we have hosted orgies for years, group play becomes a true orgy only under certain conditions. We will fully discuss them later in this book, too. *(See Chapter 9: Sex.)*

Something else to consider
By Larry

> *Nothing in life is to be feared. It is only to be understood.*
> —Marie Curie

> *The only unnatural sex act is that which you cannot perform.*
> —Alfred Kinsey

Besides the classification of activities by involvement, here is another one: by stimulation preferences. As we have mentioned before, the Lifestyle has no perverts. If you feel any of the below interests you, try it. You will likely find Lifestyle partners for whatever you have in mind.

Bondage: uses various restraints to increase sexual pleasure.
Discipline: often includes role playing, bondage, some spanking.
Sadomasochism: might be right for those of you who enjoy pain.

The three above often come together, and the common Lifestyle abbreviation for it is BDSM. The authors are not experts in any of it. Therefore, we are not in a position to give any inner classifications, descriptions, tips, or suggestions. There are specialized books on the subject you could consider as your information source if you are interested.

Swingers respect everyone's right to practice whatever is enjoyable, yet most of us are not up to real pain. (Some spanking might be fun, though!)

Nevertheless, BDSM-related activities are common enough in swinging. For instance, every Lifestyle convention we've visited has been equipped with special playrooms for BDSM people.

Straight play: Sometimes, in the Lifestyle you can hear the term "straight swingers." Straight swingers do not engage with BDSM. Straight play means painless play.

Swinging is addictive
By Larry and Mia

There is no way out!

If you decided to try swinging, you should be aware it would addict you exactly as drugs would. You will want more and more of it and you never will be able to stop. If we were in a position to invite anyone into the Lifestyle, we would certainly note on that invitation the following in uppercase:

WARNING: VERY ADDICTIVE,
YOU COULD BE OBSESSED
UNTIL THE END OF YOUR DAYS!

Some circumstances could move your Lifestyle endeavors to the back of your mind. Serious illnesses, long business trips, urgent family needs, etc., could affect your swinging activity and lead to its partial and, sometimes, complete shut down. Yet, it could happen just temporarily. Those who managed to adopt the Lifestyle philosophy and make it a part of their lives would never be able to reject it voluntarily.

If you are in the Lifestyle as a married couple, the above warning should not scare you much. Since swinging is your choice and you are happy with the way it affects your life, you should not have any complications with it. However, if your intention is to enter the Lifestyle as a single swinger (gender does not matter), reading this warning would be a good reason to consider some major implications swinging could bring into your life.

As a rule, younger single swingers do not think about their future often. Beginning from their 30s, though, they start to realize it would not be easy to find a person with whom they would be able to build a family. Closer to their 40th, some are ready to say goodbye to their matrimonial hopes.

Why does it happen? Being in the Lifestyle teaches anyone to separate love from sex, but at the same time it makes ignoring recreational sex as a major part of his/her life nearly impossible. It does not matter how strong your feelings toward some person are and how much you wish that person to become your wife or husband. If you are a swinger, you won't be capable of eliminating your swinging mindset. Therefore, you won't be able to marry anyone who is not at least a Lifestyle-friendly person.

Some of our single friends desperately try to find their future family happiness. Yet, this task is hard (if possible at all) to complete. Some, being on that assignment, try to stop swinging, most of them unsuccessfully.

Our young single friend Steve (he is 33 years old and is in the Lifestyle for 12 years) suddenly disappeared from our view. He closed his profile on the Web and did not respond to our party invitations. After a year of silence, he contacted us and told he was dating a girl and was in love with her. He also told us he was working on their first visit to swing club. He hoped to convert her into the Lifestyle and promised to be back to our parties, this time as a part of a couple. We wish him good luck!

How much does swinging cost?
By Larry

Sensual vs. financial...

Do not ever expect to participate in the Lifestyle free of charge. In fact, swinging costs a lot of money. The total depends on how deeply you are involved, how often your sensual escapades take place, and what kind of activities you prefer.

The following are just a few examples of what you would have to pay. Prices are per couple based on our experience:

Visit to a swing club $100 - $200

Add membership fees that could be up to $100 per year.

Attending a private party $40 - $150

Don't be surprised: some parties cost up to $400.

Week at Lifestyle-friendly resort $1,500 - $5,000

It differs by the week of the year and the category of the room you book.

Multi-day Lifestyle convention $800 - $1600

Date at a restaurant $80 - $150

Rent of a motel/hotel room $50 - $200

Yearly membership at swing website $70 - $180

It depends on how you prefer to pay: monthly, quarterly, or yearly.

In reality, a swing club or party visit will cost you even more. You have to bring your liquor since these events are mostly BYOB. You also have to get there and back home so you have to add transportation expenses, such as gasoline, car wear-and-tear, as well as possible tolls and parking fees.

Additionally, do not forget about transportation costs to all other events. For instance, a round-trip to Jamaica or Mexico could easily cost you over $1,000.

Let's say, you visit swing clubs or parties about once every six weeks, you have three first dates per year at the restaurant, you rent a hotel room twice a year, and once a year you vacation at a Lifestyle-friendly resort. Added together, these costs will easily take your yearly Lifestyle expenses to at least $4,000.

Anticipate this amount to grow much higher since you have to spend additional money on your Lifestyle clothes, shoes, jewelry, and accessories. Add expenditures on extra make-up, wax, manicure, and pedicure. Add overhead on specific cosmetic, beauty supplies, and fragrances. Add the cost of condoms (you will use lots of them), lubricants, gels, sex-toys, accessories, etc.

You could keep your swinging budget much lower. You could only visit free Meet & Greets and only date couples who would agree to meet you at McDonald's eateries. You could wear your everyday clothes to your dates and never visit clubs. You could also eliminate all the resorts and conventions. I have doubts you will be getting much fun in this case, though.

If you are serious enough about your participation in swinging, if you wish to experience the best of it, you should reserve about $5,000 to $6,000 as the Lifestyle part of your yearly family budget, which is a conservative estimate.

The good news is part of this money you unavoidably save by cutting on your vanilla entertainment and dining-out spending. You will have neither much time, nor interest for them once you are in the Lifestyle.

The price you pay for your adult fun is not cheap at all. Still, it is nothing compared to, for instance, a golf club membership, and, in our view, will bring more excitement into your life.

Chapter 2

Marriage and Swinging

Is swinging moral enough?
By Larry and Mia

> *When authorities warn you of the sinfulness of sex,*
> *there is an important lesson to be learned.*
> *Do not have sex with the authorities.*
> —Matt Groening

> *Why should we take advice on sex from the Pope?*
> *If he knows anything about it, he shouldn't!*
> —George Bernard Shaw

> *We should never be afraid to laugh at religion*
> *because God has a sense of humor.*
> *I realize that every time I am naked.*
> —Steven "Spanky" McFarlin

> *Sex isn't disgusting unless you make it disgusting!*
> —Bob Leander

In the vanilla world, standards of the average person or society-at-large decide for all of us what is good and what is right. Societal and religious regulations dictate how people should behave. We all have knowledge of these common moral rules and are able to distinguish right from wrong and make decisions based on that knowledge.

By our ethic, for instance, it is perfectly fine for an unmarried person to have affairs with as many people as he/she wishes to. One-by-one or at the same time, it does not matter. As long as you are single and your (single, too!) partner willingly agrees to have sex with you, you both are within our moral standards.

If you are married, however, the situation changes dramatically. Society expects you to dedicate the rest of your life to just one sex partner or else it will consider you immoral.

While we try to stay within moral bounds, that dictate does not work for many of us. What is more, it does not bring any excitement into our lives.

Many people must address a deep inner conflict here. We can call it "moral conflict," but it is much deeper than just a plain morality issue. They must either do something with their moral side or kill their sexual one. Opposite of the vanilla world, the swinging world does not have moral codes and ethic regulations. Inside the Lifestyle, the only morality that exists is "all is good that is good for you two."

Yes, we swingers still live in the vanilla world and have to cope with double standards. We are working, shopping, visiting restaurants, enjoying theaters, shows, and concerts. We are attending churches and temples. We are raising our children, taking care of our parents. Furthermore, we have vanilla friends to whom we devote some of our time. In this "normal" world, we must be discreet about swinging and behave "decently" and "honorably." Deep inside, though, we know we have achieved our true moral victory!

How to make that tough decision
By Larry

> They always say that time changes things...
> Actually, you have to change them yourself.
> —Andy Warhol

A right beginning is a half of an accomplishment.

How should you broach the whole subject of getting into the Lifestyle with your loved one? What would be the right way? No one can equip you with universal guidelines.

These questions are simple and complicated at the same time. It is simple because you know what you would like to achieve in the end—a mutual and hopefully affirmative decision. It is complicated because only the details of your relationship (often tiny enough) can possibly serve as the basis for both your strategy and tactic here. Who but you know them best?

Still, here are some recommendations you may find useful.

Your relationship must be strong enough and based on two-way trust. If it is not secure, don't even bother to start talking. You might end up in a disappointing situation. Always keep in mind that swinging is not for everyone, and keeping your relationship is more important than swinging.

You know your significant other better than anyone else and should be able to predict his/her reaction. Therefore, you are the only person who can decide what would be right—ease into it step-by-step or unload all your thoughts at once.

Our only recommendation is to do it as soon as you come to your decision. Don't wait until the situation allows you an opportunity to broach the subject; rather, create this situation yourself. You'll never know for sure unless you ask, won't you? Then just pick that moment when your partner likely is in the right mood and go for it—maybe when you two are making love, maybe while you are having a romantic dinner. If you do it the right way, the worst potential outcome will be to accept from your loved one a statement that he/she is not interested.

Here are a few real stories relevant to some of our friends' and our experiences:

Mia and I were together for more than 20 years when I had a conversation with our vanilla friend, Alan. I did not know what "vanilla" meant at the time. He was simply a friend. As we later learned, he was a swinger then and still is.

Swinging from A to Z   **33**

We were talking about Caribbean vacations, and I asked Alan, "Which island in your experience was the best?" He answered, "Jamaica, no doubt." I've heard many stories about Jamaica as well as about how unsafe for tourists this island was. I mentioned this concern to Alan. He replied, "This is all true, but you don't have to go outside the resort." I had another concern, "But it is boring to stay at the same place for the whole week!" He smiled, "Depends on the resort you are staying at."

He was talking about Hedonism II (nicknamed Hedo), which he had visited five times. I was intrigued, so I started reading comments and articles about Hedo on the Web. Then I first realized the swinging Lifestyle really exists. Previously, we thought of swingers as some insignificant group of freaks and perverts who enjoy abnormal and immoral things. We could not even imagine us being a part of this group. Yet, I thought that visiting Hedo and looking at what all these people were all about was worth a try.

Since Mia and I were always in a strong and trusting relationship based on love, true friendship, and mutual respect, I brought this idea to her. One day, in bed after making love, I told her about Alan's suggestion and shared with her the results of my Hedo research. She was interested and agreed that we should go. I remember asking, "If we go there, do you realize it would be a waste of time and money if we would not get naked from the first minute we are there?" She agreed. I continued, "Do you agree it would be a good idea of not being opposed upfront to some action we might be willing to participate in?" She agreed again. Next, I remember telling her how I would love to watch her having sex with other men. She responded she would also like to see me with other women.

At that time, we both were so aroused we started having sex again. For both of us that sex was as if we performed it with someone we never knew before. We began to open unknown sexual sides in each other right away. In fact, we started swinging long before we encountered our first actual partners swap. That minute changed our life forever.

We agreed to free our minds and go with the flow, leaving all the details and possible concerns for later resolution. "We'll cross the bridge when we come to it" is an important assumption for want-to-be-swingers.

Sure, we had some minor (and not that minor) issues along the way, but we've managed to sort all of them out, one by one. The only thing we are still frustrated about is that Alan did not tell us about Hedo 10 years earlier!

Our friends Tony and Lucille have been married for 19 years, but they have been swinging for two months more than they have been married. They started while still engaged. Once they were watching a sexual scene in a TV movie—a guy with two girls having a threesome. Lucille joked about how she would like to see Tony with two girls and not even be one of them. Tony replied he would gladly do that, but only after seeing her with two guys. What was just a joke became their first swing club visit. Tony was jealous over Lucille at first, but lost his jealousy after their wedding took place.

Other friends, Al and Grace, gave swinging a try too. Al told us the following:

"We were together for 12 years and were secure in our relationship. More than that, we were real friends. Still, I was not quite sure about Grace's reaction when I once told her, 'Listen, I would not want to become old and weak before we could even try having sex with other people. I mean both of us. The fact that we are a loving and fully trusting couple does not suggest we have to be just each other's lovers until the end of our days. A lot of nice men are around for you to be with as well as many women for me! And we could do it together!' I remember unloading it all in one shot, nervously waiting for her reaction. What a huge relief it was to hear that Grace shared my desire and had thought about it a few times herself. We started from opening a profile at a swing website and dating couples privately. Now we are fully in the Lifestyle for more than a year."

Our friend Lame, of Bruce and Lame, a couple in their late 40s who we often meet at swing clubs, told us the following tale:

"Once we were watching porn, a scene with two girls playing with each other. Bruce asked, 'Sweetie, would you like to be in bed with some other woman and allow me to watch you both having sex?' I remember answering I would have nothing against it. We did not know anything about swinging then and, frankly, we even did not think about having fun with another couple, much less multiple couples at once. All we decided to do was attempt to find a girl for me, just for girl-to-girl fun. We tried to find someone on a regular dating website and through newspaper ads but did not succeed. Bruce did some research and discovered a swing website where we opened a profile stating we were looking for a single woman. However, we did not make it even there. Although, what we were able to do was to find another couple with similar interests. After meeting this couple for dinner at a restaurant, we moved to their apartment, and it happened. I played with the other woman while both our husbands watched. Though I expected more from this experience than I got, I still was excited, and we decided to continue our experiments.

"We dated a few more couples under the same conditions. Once we visited a swing club. We didn't find a single girl there, but we had unbelievable sex with each other. At that time, we realized we enjoy people around watching us while we are having sex. It was a huge turn on for us. The first step led to the second and, finally, we had our first full-swap. It happened two years ago. Now we settle for nothing less. I still love to play with girls, but, in the end, I need a decent man to bring me to orgasm, or better, two men! Besides, I love watching Bruce with other women. We never suspected swinging was what we needed!"

What are the initial options?
By Larry and Mia

>*My family never raised me to have a vagina.*
>*—Roseanne*

> *What do I know about sex? I'm a married man.*
> —Tom Clancy

> *Whatever you can do or dream you can do it, begin it.*
> *Boldness has genius, power, and magic to it.*
> —Goethe

While the water is still shallow...

Okay, you have managed to reach *that* agreement. You both decided to try it, and you are determined and curious at the same time. Now you've come to the point of actually doing it.

Someone once told us, "Swinging is like getting into cold water. Getting there inch-by-inch takes a long time to get comfortable. Jumping right in makes you feel good in no time at all." This expression is nice, yet, unfortunately, useless. Following this approach could work for some beginners while it would destroy the swinging intentions for others. Apparently, an opposite recommendation, "Take it slow!" would not be helpful to everyone as well. Let us repeat this: everything about swinging should be comfortable to both of you and must be your own decision.

The following are common ways to test the waters:

Visiting a swing club would be your easiest option. We will talk about clubs, their types, common activities, and appropriate behavior later. Swing clubs are a huge branch of the swinging Lifestyle and require a separate discussion. *(See Chapter 6: Meeting Others in Person.)*

If you are lucky to reside in an area with nude beaches, you could try them, too. Not many nudists are swingers, but many (if not most) swingers are nudists. Chances are you will meet your first dates there.

Often, Lifestyle newcomers are afraid to visit a swing club or nude beach because of the possibility of meeting someone there who knows them in the vanilla world: friends, co-workers, neighbors, etc. We were afraid, too.

At one of our first club visits, Mia met a man who was working in the same building where her office was. With no hesitation at all, he gave her a business card and asked her to call him if we would ever wish to meet him and his wife for some adult fun.

Our friend Nick, an investment banker who has a well-established and successful business, told us this story:

"Once I was visiting a swing club with my fiancée when I spotted my business partner entering the door with his wife. All four of us knew each other well. We were friends in our vanilla life. It did not take long for them to pick us out of the crowd as well. What happened next is we all just pretended we didn't know each other, and nobody left the scene! We all had lots of fun and just avoided being too close. We've never mentioned this incident afterward. We are still partners and vanilla friends more than 10 years after it happened."

The reality is swingers are discreet people who would never be interested in reporting their Lifestyle contacts to the vanilla world. If they do, they gain nothing besides revealing themselves as swingers.

Don't be afraid of meeting your vertical friends or acquaintances in the Lifestyle.

The following comes from our friends Simon and Lori:

"We were at our favorite swing club when we suddenly met our best vanilla friends there. We had just left their house where we had had dinner with them a few hours ago! We never suspected they were swingers. Well, they are our *really* best friends since."

Here is another story. It has nothing to do with clubs, but still relates to the issue. We met a young, attractive couple, Sam and Lucy, through the Web. They were beginners; in fact, we were firsts for them. Nevertheless, we had some good-quality adult fun together several times. Once they asked us to introduce them to our other friends. We knew a couple, Michael and Millie, who lived in the same area as Sam and Lucy and decided to bring them together. One day, we invited both couples to our house, and the minute they met we learned they were already friends in the vanilla world. Furthermore, Sam and Lucy were amazed to learn that their other common vanilla friends were swingers, too. They all were laughing the whole evening—apparently, no one was frustrated with their discoveries.

If you wish to be as private as possible and start from dating other couples or singles, the option you should consider is opening a profile on a swing website. This approach worked fine for several our friends, including Sam and Lucy. Besides providing you with an opportunity to contact other swingers, websites give you a wide range of other information, such as about meet-and-greets, hotel and private parties, clubs, swing conventions, etc., in your area as well as nationwide. We will discuss such websites later in this book. *(See Chapter 5: Meeting on the Internet.)*

Meet-and-greet is also a popular activity among beginners since it provides them with the option of being acquainted with many people at once instead of meeting one couple at a time.

Another good idea for the beginners is vacationing at Hedo or other swinger-friendly resorts, such as Desire in Cancun or Caliente in Tampa and Puerto Plata. Meet real swingers, experience the true freedom of being naked on a beach, join others at wild theme parties with all those crazy revealing outfits, perform dirty dancing at discos, watch open sexual activities, and figure what is right and what is wrong for you. At these places you can define your level of involvement without pressure and concern of feeling judged. That's where our own starting point was, and it worked for us. The biggest pro in starting swinging at such a resort is the friendly environment that is only possible at places like these. The biggest con? This kind of vacation is not cheap.

Never try bringing your partner to these resorts without a pre-established mutual agreement, though, or you may risk your relationship. On our third trip to Hedo, we witnessed a couple in their early 40s having loud arguments in the lobby. They had just checked in. The first thing they spotted on the way to their room was *naked people!* She was in shock and insisted on leaving for home immediately. Apparently, the husband hadn't told his wife what to expect. Finally, the Hedo manager offered to transfer them to another resort. They agreed and pompously left the battle scene.

The Lifestyle is all about sharing
By Larry

Give some and have some, too.

Sharing is one of the most important Lifestyle assumptions. Indeed, you should not expect another swinging couple to allow you to play with just one of them. They will expect an appropriate exchange.

As you know, a swinging couple is a basic Lifestyle component, and most of the time it is not breakable into smaller units, that is, man and woman separately. Exceptions exist, of course, but, in this case, we would talk about "pseudo" couples; for instance, two singles who agree to temporarily form a couple for both of them to get into a couples-only club or party.

If you wish to play with someone who is a part of a couple, you must *share* your partner with his/her partner as well. You can't avoid sharing.

Each of you has to be fair to each other. Do not expose your loved one to a possibility of playing with a person he/she would not like to play with. Always ask your partner about his or her feelings regarding particular couples even before you approach them. If you both are good enough in executing the "doing one for the team" technique *(see Chapter 3: Dating Couples)*, you will have a lot of fun. Still, approaching another couple (or part of that couple) without a prior arrangement with your own partner may mean making the only person important to you to sacrifice and suffer needlessly. Nothing good comes from it.

Sharing in the Lifestyle has another meaning that is not obvious. Sharing your partner with others also means additional sexual energy re-distribution between you two, this time on a much deeper emotional level. Indeed, you still share your fun, your feelings, your emotions, and your desires right through your playmates. You share your energy with the other couple and absorb their energy in return. Both couples are *charging* from each other, and everyone uses this additional energy as a resource for their own intimate upgrade. The result: most people start to notice improvements in their sexuality after a short time in the Lifestyle.

After becoming swingers, we turned into different people sexually. For instance, Mia *now* and Mia *before* are two different women. Just to name a few points, Mia *now* is bi, she is multi-orgasmic, she squirts sometimes, and she is able to give the best "deep throat" any man ever could dream about. None of these sexual qualities existed just a few years ago. More than that, she herself did not have the slightest idea any of them ever applied to her. Thank you, Lifestyle, for making us one of the happiest couples on this planet. Our dreams came true.

Proper safety measures
By Larry & Mia

Never leave home without condoms!

Fear of exposure to STDs is one of major factors keeping people from having sex outside their relationships. No doubt, it significantly reduces the frequency of extra-marital affairs.

Worries, uncertainties, and concerns—all of these STD-related aspects are widespread in the Lifestyle even more than in the vanilla world. None of us can ignore this matter since swinging is all about having sex with strangers. Some risk is the price of the fun.

You would not trust anyone telling you swinging is completely risk-free, and you would be right. At the same time, a reality might sound surprising for you. The chances of possible exposure to STDs in the Lifestyle are significantly lower compared with the vanilla world. Yes, we swingers frequently engage in recreational sexual activities. Yes, the average swinger has more bodily contacts than an average vanilla person does. Yet, swingers are safer, and the following are the reasons why.

First, most swingers are married couples. We do not cheat on each other with the kind of vanilla people, who are morally and physically open to sex with virtually everyone. We do not engage in sex with male and female prostitutes of any kind. Instead, we only have sex with other married couples whose sexual behavior is similar to ours.

Second, safe sex is favored and enforced in the Lifestyle. Yet, if someone plays bareback (the authors have not met many), they will tell you about their preference well in advance, and it will be up to you to decline (we always do).

Third, swingers take good care of themselves. Most of us take showers after sex as well as before it and use special disinfecting shampoos. In the vanilla environment, you can catch an STD and have no idea for years as long as it takes place without open symptoms. (Some venereal infections do not pop up on the surface.) However, the same situation is hardly possible within the Lifestyle since swingers perform checkups more often than vanilla people do. If you are active, we recommend such testing at least every other month.

Three words best expressing what you are simply obligated to use in terms of your safety are condoms, condoms, and condoms! Do not count on the party hosts or someone else to supply them; always have your own. Take with you more than your bravest hopes would require.

We have our designated "swing bag" where we keep all the Lifestyle necessities when we go out. Besides, Larry's outfits often lack pockets and his cigarettes, lighter, car keys, and a driver's license go there too. We always have two dozen condoms in this bag. We replenish after each party we attend.

A suitable level of risk you can afford depends on you and you only. For instance, oral play in the Lifestyle is commonly unprotected. However, we met some people who insisted on using condoms for that part of the fun, too. In our experience, others never turned them down just because of these requirements.

You can also decrease the risk by avoiding connections with single swingers and pseudo-couples. Our single friends are true swingers who, in turn, date swingers only. Therefore, we can reasonably trust them. You should apply your "rule of suspicion" first to those who are new for you and do not have referrals from your friends.

Here is one more tip. Do not trust people who claim they are tested and are STD-free. Yes, they may have had a checkup. They may have a freshly issued certificate to show. Moreover, they may truly believe they are disease-free. However, do you know how many people they played with since their last test? Nobody could give you 100% assurance in any situation.

The danger is always there. The question is just how much of it you are ready to accept. Hence, you are never *completely* safe. You can only be *reasonably* safe.

Chapter 3

Dating Couples

A couple is the core Lifestyle measurement unit
By Larry

A couple makes the [swinging] world go around.

Swinging is all about couples. Let us stress it again—a couple is what makes and moves the Lifestyle.

It doesn't matter whether you are at a swing club, house party, hotel party, or on a private date with another couple. In all cases, you can be sure—everyone in the Lifestyle acknowledges you as a *duo* rather than two people, man and woman *separately*. Other swingers measure you by your common personality, pooled intelligence, joint appearance, summary aura, mutual charm, and combined sexual appeal. Please note up front, not everyone will be able to form his or her judgment on you right away. Yet have no doubt, a combination of all these factors will constitute a basis for your "evaluation" by others.

The most complicated part of a couple-to-couple swinging relationship is this so-called *click* that must happen between all of you even before you are able to agree on having common sensual fun. It does not matter what kind of activities we are talking about here. Regardless if you are soft-swappers or full-swappers, you still would not want to play with people you don't like, would you?

Let's assume for a minute that you are a single person, not a part of a couple. What are the odds you would wish to have sex with the other particular person? Your answer will depend on many factors, including the given person's appearance and several other qualities playing an important role for you. Every one of us has his/her individual model of perfection or, at least, attractiveness. For you to decide, you would compare the person in question with this model and judge by the result of this process. You wouldn't like everyone, and, therefore, the possibility will never be 100%. In fact, it will never be even 50%, rather much less.

But you are a couple trying to connect with the other swinging couple, and we are talking about odds for all four of you!

You can counter, "Wait a second, but I (the man) do not need to match another couple's husband. And my wife is not bisexual; she does not have to match his wife since she would be only playing with the man himself."

You would be wrong! Since you *dedicate* your partner to the other person, it *does matter* how you connect with that person yourself. Mia, for instance, would never approve a couple where the woman's energy appears to her as negative. As for me, I would be far from happy seeing my better half with some man whom I do not like, for any reason. Remember, swinging must be fun for both of you, together, as a couple.

Back to odds, how much less are they for a couple-to-couple click compared to a single-to-single one? Well, the theory of statistics teaches us that the chances for two-by-two interactions are at least eight times less than for one-by-one!

The reality is you could hardly find another couple for a swinging relationship, which all four of you would *equally* enjoy. For all our time in the Lifestyle, we have met so far only two couples who are our complete and ideal match. Should you wait for that excellent equality to happen and only allow yourselves to play in this case? No, you should not. If you enter swinging with the intention of spending the rest of your life in search of the perfection, you will easily end your days being Lifestyle virgins.

At each encounter, one of you (or better, both) has to slim down individual criteria to some extent to keep your performance as a couple alive. This downscaling could allow your partner to have fun even if you would not get as much pleasure this time as you would like to. Swingers had established this practice well and often refer to it as "doing one for the team."

Doing one for the team
By Larry

> Neither sex gets its ideal mate all the time; choice becomes a compromise between what one wants and what is available.
> —Mary Batten

And the winner is...

The ultimate truth is couples who ascertain the "doing one for the team" concept and execute this theory well are the most successful in the Lifestyle.

Since perfect matches are rare, you would want to begin with establishing your own version of the above concept.

Nobody in the Lifestyle will judge you by your swinging interests, preferences, and the way you make them a reality. You are the only ones who can decide what is acceptable and what is not. Therefore, the authors are not in a position to define it for you. All we can help with is to suggest a few thoughts on the matter.

First, you have to establish the lowest reasonable point of your approval criteria. Find out how much each of you is able to downscale his/her individual model of sex partner acceptance. The higher this point, the lower the possibility of playing with the couple in question. And vice versa: the more each of you is ready to sacrifice, the better your chances are.

So, where is the border between "they are worth a try" and "we are not into them?" It resides inside of you two as a couple. You have to feel it.

For beginners, set your bar as high as you wish. You can drop it inch-by-inch as you go. Trust us: this bar will be tumbling by itself as you both gain experience and a strong belief in yourselves as a Lifestyle couple. Still, if either of you gives up too much while making your first steps in swinging, it is possible to end up with the feeling of *being used* that, in turn, leads to frustration and, sometimes, depression.

You might decide this disappointment is your partner's fault (it is not). The outcome may be catastrophic for your relationship. Such a situation can introduce serious problems. Even if you can resolve them, they still might become a sufficient reason to stop swinging altogether. We know some couples who did.

We did not swing for long when we invited Ike and Lorraine to our place. We had been chatting with them on a swing website for a while. I liked Lorraine the first minute they entered the house. After an hour or so of talking and giggling, I was eager to start the action. It seemed like our guests, a more experienced couple, were ready, too. However, Mia, taking a minute with me privately, asked me to call the date off, as she did not feel attracted to them at all. Instead of giving Ike and Lorraine our apologies and sending them home, I started asking my wife to change her mind. Among other arguments, I told her it would not be polite to our guests. Being a nice person and loving wife, Mia finally agreed.

As soon as our guests left, Mia started crying and blamed me for using her. I was shocked. I thought everything was fine as long as she agreed to play. Apparently, we both were wrong in our assumptions. Mia overestimated her own ability to handle situations like that. As for me, I should have never pushed her.

What was the end of it? Mia hated me for three days. We did not talk for a week. As for our next Lifestyle getaway, it happened in two months, rather every other week as it happened before. Thanks to our strong and trusting relationship, we survived, but we still remember this painful story in every detail. When we later met Ike and Lorraine at a hotel party, we ran out.

Surprisingly, the situation that happened to us has its own Lifestyle term as well. Swingers call it to be "burned." Yes, that couple burned us!

We conclude:
- Never be nice to your partner by doing anything that you are not comfortable with.
- Never agree to having fun with someone if you are positive that you don't like the idea.
- Never insist on anything if you can see your partner is not up to it.
- Never be afraid to upset another couple. Their possible frustration is incomparable with what could occur to you.

Could anything like the above happen to us now, when we are "seasoned"? No! We are set in our ways and have done a lot of swinging; we have been in different situations, some good, some not so good. Best of all, we know each other in all the tiniest details. We can handle any setting and go to the end with virtually anyone, no matter who they are and what we feel about them. Yet, we could do so on one condition only—if *both of us* would like to!

Again and again, swinging must be fun. Don't let anyone and anything turn your fun into a misery. Do anything in your power to avoid feeling burned; it's so painful!

Another major part of "doing one for the team" is an ability to save your possibly more or less negative emotions for yourself. You should be able to keep smiling and stay reasonably happy, at least on the surface. You have to be a good actor on the swinging stage and deliberately play your role as a part of your mutual performance as a couple.

Gentlemen, did you ever fake orgasms? Sometimes you'll need to. If you want your better half to have a good time while being satisfied, sometimes you will have to fake your feelings, emotions, and even orgasms to support mutual fun.

The good news is that doing one for the team feature, when employed correctly, has two-way traffic. You might stay less satisfied today but become entirely happy tomorrow in return.

With time in swinging, your individual models of partner acceptance change dramatically and both of you begin enjoying situations you never enjoyed before. You realize, for example, that sexual satisfaction depends least on how your play partners look.

Some swinging activities (for instance, threesomes) do not require the "doing one for the team" approach. However, anything involving couples requires you to be a true team. Remember, it is hardly possible to play with the person you like without *sharing* your own partner with that person's one!

The only exception from this rule is a *true orgy* where everyone plays for himself or herself *(see Chapter 9: Sex)*. However, the reality is that you would not be able to start swinging right from there due to several major factors, including your inexperience in couple-to-couple play. Orgy is Lifestyle's top of the line; you have to be somewhat mature to feel comfortable enough and be able to perform there decently.

Setting the rules
By Larry and Mia

> *Whether you think you can, or whether you think you can't, either way you're right.*
> —Henry Ford

> *The appetite grows by eating.*
> —Rabelais

In addition to defining aspects of "doing one for the team," you would want to establish your internal swinging rules. These rules do not only relate to couple-to-couple play. You can have a separate set of rules for each type of activity.

First, these rules should accommodate your thoughts about your swinging behavior as a couple. Second, they should consider both of you as individuals. This way you will feel at ease and eliminate unwanted concerns before they get you in trouble. As always, the only criteria is that swinging should be fun.

Sit together for a while and think about what you both would like and what would not like your partner to do. Put your thoughts on paper, walk through them two or three more times to correct and enhance, memorize, and take these rules seriously. From now on they become "traffic laws" that both of you must strictly follow. That's how you will assess and confirm your mutual trust. The level of this trust will grow or decline depending on your performance under these rules.

Do not take rules you've just defined as set in stone, though. You will modify them as you gain swinging experience. Despite that, always follow the rules exactly as you *currently* formulated them. Being in the slightest violation means (at minimum) upsetting your partner, and he/she is the only person who is significant.

After being in the Lifestyle for more than 15 years, our friends Roland and Nadine have ended up with only three rules, in this order:

1. Nadine goes first.
2. Do not embarrass Nadine.
3. Do not be greedy, share.

As for us, we only have one left, "Don't ask me twice." Meaning, we never try to change each other's decision related to any single aspect of the given situation and behave accordingly. It works perfectly.

First dates

By Larry and Mia

Make hay while the sun shines.

Let's assume, you are in full agreement regarding your upcoming activities and you have set your internal rules. You know exactly where your current boundaries are, both of you are ready to play one for the team. Finally, you are at the point of meeting a couple who might be your good match. Is all the above enough to achieve your expectations? The answer is still "No."

The important rules for first dates are:
- Never anticipate people you date to be perfect. They likely aren't.
- Never expect in advance that your dates will accept you. They have the right to decline you exactly as you have that same right. Be honest with yourselves; you are not perfect, either.
- Never feel obligated. Never think you owe your dates anything just because you agreed to meet with them. Don't be afraid to say "No."
- Always remember, no one, if he/she is a real swinger, will expect you to play with him/her unless you like the idea.
- Never feel frustrated if your date is unsuccessful. Just move on without hard feelings. Other dates will follow shortly.
- Try to make up your mind as soon as possible, at least while you are still on that date. We do not suggest you grab everyone right away. You still should apply your criteria, but try to get to your mutual decision while your dates are still available and willing to play with you, or else you can easily lose them. Not every couple will agree to gamble away their time meeting you repeatedly for you to "get closer."

While we were making our first steps in the Lifestyle, we came up with some sign language idea that allowed us to exchange our thoughts about people we meet even without talking to each other. While at the restaurant table with our dates, we did not have to excuse ourselves and walk out to discuss our thoughts and possible next steps. We actually had just five established signs meaning "I like him," "I like her," "I like them both," "Let's do it," and the most important, "Get out of here before it's too late!"

You could use this idea, too. For instance, with one touch of your left ear with your right hand ("Let's call it off"), you could end your date and say goodbye even before ordering dessert, and save some money, too!

Do we use those signs now? No, we don't. We even forgot what they were—another illustration on how time spent in the Lifestyle causes people to evolve.

The function of the date in the Lifestyle is different from one in the vanilla world. It is not about being two-on-two instead of one-on-one. It is rather about the outcome we try to achieve. In the vanilla world, we are looking for some kind of relationship, while in the Lifestyle our sole purpose is sexual fun, often just a one-night stand. Still, the date is necessary because only personal contact could give us a complete and absolute impression that would serve as an objective basis for our decision in every case.

Not everything always goes as planned at the first date. Be prepared for some surprises that other couples might present to you.

On one of our first dates (our sign language did not exist yet), we were meeting a couple, Greg and Ronnie. We agreed to meet at their favorite restaurant. They told us how beautiful the place was and how delicious the meals were. We left on time, but due to traffic conditions, arrived about 20 minutes later than planned. We knew for sure they were already inside waiting for us since we called from the car to let them know we were running late.

When we entered the place, four or five tables were taken. Only two of them were occupied by couples, and none of these couples looked like Greg and Ronnie. We stayed at the door wondering what was happening when one of those couples spotted us and invited to their table with warm smiles. Those were Greg and Ronnie! We saw pictures of them they sent us and, according to those pictures and their website profile, expected to see a nice-looking couple of age 44 and 42. Reality was different. They were in their late 50s. They sent us pictures that were at least 15 years old.

What would we do now if we suddenly found ourselves in these circumstances? We would just thank our dates for their time and drive back home. Yet, those days we were newbies and thought it would be rude to express what we felt about the situation they planted us in. Besides, we were starving.

We had dinner with them while listening to endless stories about his success in business, his Corvette, and his great physical condition. After paying about $150 for a dinner we did not enjoy, we found ourselves in the parking lot, stuck between his famous Corvette and our car, and responding to an invitation to go straight to their house. We knew, even without our sign language, our only desire was to leave as soon as possible. We don't recall exactly what we told them, something like we were not ready to play *that* night, promised to call them in a few days, and left.

We did not call them, and they did not call us afterward. Yet, in about two weeks, being nice, we sent an e-mail thanking them for a beautiful evening and "superb" dinner at the "positively splendid" restaurant. We wrote we liked them as people (their "deep intellect," "perfect manners," etc.), but we did not feel like we could become their play partners. Their answer stated they understood they are not "everyone's cup of Earl Grey." Still, they were glad we liked the restaurant and the food. They also wrote something about their strong belief in "truth in advertising" and that they would never promote anything that is not true.

Truth in advertising, my ass! We never understood what certain people try to achieve by lying about their real age. Could Greg and Ronnie *really* think those antique pictures would help them in their playmates search?

For your date, make sure to be on time. At least call people you are dating to let them know if you are running late. Don't make others wait for you. Everyone is different, but no one gets positive emotions from your being late. Some would be frustrated, while others could get mad. In any case, your chances to connect with other people would not get any better.

Remember, reliability is the key, and in the Lifestyle, it is even more important compared with the vanilla world. In both cases, unreliable people cause a waste of time, but when it comes to swinging, they waste the most valuable one—time reserved for fun!

We never wait for anyone for more than five minutes. If people did not come and did not call, they are out, simply like that. Moreover, we will never consider them as our prospective dates again. We make sure people we meet know about this policy upfront, so no surprises. Our fun time is important to us. We are not up to gambling on it. Many friends of ours have the same or similar policy.

We used to date couples and still do. However, after having a few negative experiences and a few when our dates did not show up at all, we've decided to stop dating at public places. Our current first date policy is to only meet at swing clubs and swing parties.

Why did we decide to go this way? Because this approach eliminates misuse of fun time. It also comes up much cheaper. We don't have to pay for dinners and drinks that lead nowhere. It takes care of our possible frustration, too. If we did not click with our dates, many others are around we can connect and play with right away. What is most important, though, is we don't feel any obligations and do not have to push ourselves to play just because no one else would be available to us tonight.

The concept of meeting prospective playmates at Lifestyle events rather than at public places gives us yet another benefit: we can meet virtually every couple who contacted us despite their look, age, swinging preferences, etc. Besides, we don't have to care about their pictures at all. We usually forgo exchanging pictures with the exception of a single face shot so we may recognize each other when we meet.

Swing clubs and swing parties provide us with an obligation-free environment that helps us figure out our next steps right away. We are there to have adult fun while the date we scheduled is an added benefit. If we click with our dates, we can play right away. Otherwise, both parties are free to move on and still have more than enough opportunities for the night.

Another reality we have bumped into after years in the Lifestyle is that we never know what our reaction will be until we are able to observe people in person. Sometimes, we meet people who are not attractive physically, but are appealing emotionally, intellectually, and sexually. These qualities, in our view, compensate fully for all their appearance deficiencies and result in additional advantages in the end. At the same time, we also met a lot of great-looking people and experienced huge turnoffs after they opened their mouths.

As it is said, "Beauty is in the eye of beholder." Alternatively, as one of our friends likes to rephrase it, "Beauty is in the eye of the beer holder."

Not every couple is ready for the club scene and group parties, though. Many swingers don't do anything but private couple-to-couple dating. Therefore, if you would come to the same conclusion as we did, you could significantly reduce the number of new people whom you would be able to meet. The decision is up to you.

Swinging and friendship
By Larry

Don't overcook it!

You've finally managed to find that *right* couple and have played with them. Congratulations!

No matter where this fun has happened, at the club, hotel room, or someone's house, you either liked it or not. If you enjoyed it enough and still don't have your playmates' contact information, right afterward would be the right time to ask. You might want to play with them again. If they took pleasure in their time with you as well, they will give it to you, and will ask for yours in return. By the way, this question is the best way to know if the satisfaction was mutual.

When sharing contact information, never reveal to anyone the telephone number of your better half. You don't know these people well enough yet, do you? Then do yourselves a favor. Protect your lady from weird calls. We heard enough stories where men of the couples tried to convince the other couple's women to one-on-one dates. One of these men literally terrorized a woman. He threatened to call her husband and tell him they had already met and had sex if she refused to meet him.

How often should you meet your new horizontal friends? How should you build your swinging relationship with these people for you to enjoy and maximize all the possible benefits?

The most common mistake in this case is getting too close. Inexperienced swingers usually have the tendency to think a swinging friendship should be nothing but the equivalent of a vanilla friendship. They acknowledge the Lifestyle term "friends with benefits"; however, in most cases, they approach it incorrectly.

Please be aware: as soon as you start sharing with your swinging partners your private thoughts and open them any sides of your personal life not directly related to sex, you are getting into trouble. In a best-case scenario, you will obtain new vanilla friends. In the worst case, the situation might grow to be complicated and even dangerous. Anyway, having these people as a playmates becomes somewhat convoluted. In addition, it can be the most efficient way to end your swinging relationship with them.

We met Leo and Trisha at a private house party, played with them, and somewhat liked it. It was not the best encounter of our lives. Still, it was decent. Besides, they both were nice, intelligent people, and they seemed attracted to us as well. In three weeks, we had them at a small party in our house. A short time later, they invited us to their place where we met their other friends, Ned and Ellen. At the time, these four were extremely close. They lived a few blocks from each other and met often. Ned and Ellen were in the Lifestyle for a relatively long time, and Leo and Trisha were newbies. We were only their third or fourth couple.

We had good-quality fun that night with everyone and left for home in the morning. In a couple days, Trisha called to invite us to a flower exhibition and a dinner in some restaurant afterward. We were not interested in those kinds of activities and declined, saying we had other plans.

They called a week later asking us to travel with them to a vanilla event in the other city. We declined again using some other reason.

The next call from them we received in another couple of weeks. This time, they intended to book a two-bedroom suite at a nice suburban hotel for a long weekend. As they said, they would be happy if we could join them there for the whole three days, just the four of us, "having the time of our lives." I remember saying we would gladly meet them, but only for sex and not for any other occasion. For us, it did not make any sense to put vanilla and Lifestyle activities in the same basket. We did not need to have vanilla fun with swingers; we had enough vanilla friends for that.

They stopped calling us. We did not call them either. Some time later, we noticed they removed their profile from the swing website. In a couple of months, we met their friends Ned and Ellen at a private party. They told us they agreed to get away with Leo and Trisha to that hotel for the long weekend. (We did not tell them about our invitation.)

Leo and Trisha had tried to make this getaway something romantic and memorable—see some sights, visit a local museum, play tennis, have dinner, etc. Ned and Ellen followed them the whole first day and got so exhausted, they were not up to any sexual activities at all.

Early the next morning Leo tried to wake them up for the same kind of "fun," but Ned and Ellen said they wanted to sleep in. When they got up in a couple of hours, Leo and Trisha were gone without leaving a note. That was the end of their swinging relationship.

Evidently, Leo and Trisha came to swinging with wrong expectations. They expected to establish links incompatible with the Lifestyle and find partners for everything all at once. They attempted to make vanilla friends out of swingers and yet tried to keep swinging with them. After they realized they couldn't, they lost interest in swinging.

Many newcomers in the Lifestyle do not realize how swinging should work and, in fact, the only way it can work.

Many ads and website profiles state, "We are not looking for just sex; we are looking for long-term friendship based on sex," "Friendship comes first, sex second," etc. Whoever stands beyond these ads believes having sex with strangers doesn't work. They think they would only be able to perform with people after knowing them better, meeting multiple times, going to movies and theaters, having dinners, and so on.

An alert for you: these people are either inexperienced (the best case), may have some kind of family drama, or have tried swinging and failed. Or else, they are just fakes pretending to be real swingers. In some cases, those are just the husbands alone who are eager to convert their wives into the Lifestyle against their will. They are trying to convince their better halves to start from something just for the sake of starting and they would gladly use you in their effort if you give them a chance.

Friendship based on sex does not exist. Sex and friendship are separate and contradictory items in the menu. It is unlikely that sex would come out of friendship. Friendship, in turn, *can* come from sexual relations, but only *Lifestyle* friendship, not the vanilla variety. Exceptions are rare.

Getting too close can make sexual relationships beyond your marriage weird. The following story comes from Cin of Rob and Cin, a couple we often meet at our favorite swing club.

"When we were just starting our Lifestyle journey, we met a couple and were attracted to each other from our very first date. We started meeting almost every weekend. Their only son was already married and lived separately, so their house was where we all had fun. Our affair was about three months old when they invited us to spend the whole weekend together. After we all had fun in the bed, the other wife asked, 'Why don't we spend the night in separate bedrooms? I would love to be with Rob the whole night alone.' Rob looked at me, silently asking for my approval. That was out of the rules we had established with this couple. We only agreed to have fun in the same room, and they knew that.

"Suddenly, I felt so bad. She wanted Rob all for herself, and he was ready to go for it. Both this couple and my husband betrayed me. I am sweet and nice to people in person, but, at that time, something unusual happened to me. I stood up and said to Rob, 'Honey, I almost forgot, we need to run home. We have an unexpected appointment with our landscaper early in the morning we could not possibly miss.' We said goodbye and left. Obviously, we never saw that couple again."

Cin did the right thing. She resolved the problem even before it occurred, thanks to her strong personality. Yet, the true core of the whole issue was not in her, her husband, or the other couple's better half. They got *too close* to each other, and the outcome was that one of them thought everything was possible, even breaking the mutual agreement.

Here is the story of Rich and Janice told to us by Janice:

"A couple of years ago, we had a pretty intense relationship with the other swinging couple for four to five months. We got so close with them, we could not think about dating someone else. At that time, I began noticing that Lucy, wife of that couple, suddenly started behaving somewhat oddly. She looked at me as if I were her enemy. It was clear; she became jealous of her husband. At the same time, she had nothing against having sex with mine. Her husband had noticed this attitude too, or maybe they had some talk on the subject. Anyway, sex was not that good anymore. In fact, it was not good at all, at least for me. Finally, Rich and I decided to end this relationship with our friends."

Rich and Janice were lucky to get rid of their ties with those people quickly enough. Things could get much worse otherwise. One more item to emphasize is that other's internal problems aren't yours (as well as yours aren't theirs). Let others resolve their issues themselves. Keep your distance.

Here is another story, this time our own. One of those two *perfect* matches we have mentioned above is David and Rosette. Our common friends brought them to our house a couple of years ago. Since all four of us tremendously liked each other, we started to meet as often as possible. We did not give up hosting our own and visiting other parties and swing clubs, yet we were together with them at most, if not all, of these events. We even went to Hedo and Desire together, and we always absolutely enjoyed our time together.

Our swinging relationship with David and Rosette was so perfect that Mia and I became frightened something may happen to it at some point. We decided that being protective in this case would be best. As a result, we had that not easy conversation with our best Lifestyle friends and convinced them to reduce the frequency of our encounters. We are still happy with each other while meeting just about once a month and intend to keep it this way.

The authors would recommend against concentrating on just one couple, even if this couple is the best you could ever imagine. Intensity in a swinging relationship is not the ideal way of doing things. We are far from discouraging couple-to-couple swinging relationships, yet would advise to take them as slow as possible. Don't get close to anyone and don't let anyone get close to you. If you wish, make the couple in question your priority, but do not substitute the whole variety of fun the Lifestyle offers with just one relationship.

The whole philosophy of swinging is all about new experiences and, therefore, new people, new partners. Metaphorically, it is about "fresh meat." The wider the variety of your swinging activities, the more complete your satisfaction will be. What's the point to be into swinging if you substitute one long-term relationship, your own, with another long-term one, with so-called "friends"?

Friendship and swinging
By Mia

One old friend is better than two new ones.
—Russian proverb

In the last section, we attempted to establish why the idea of making friends out of swingers would be dangerous. This section is about the opposite: trying to convert vanilla friends into the Lifestyle ones.

We were making our first swinging steps then. Our close vanilla friends, Alden and Millry, were spending the night at our country house. They had spent nights at our home before. However, this time, after dinner when we all got drunk enough, we ended up in the swimming pool naked. I don't recall who exactly brought up the idea, but it worked! To skip straight to the point, we had sex with them that night, and that was a full-swap. The next morning was less exciting. Millry was ashamed and felt bad. She could not look at us. Alden smiled, but clearly was not his normal self. They left earlier than usual.

We did not stop calling each other afterward, but something was odd between us since. We met in about a month, this time at their place, and we had sex again. It was as if we'd met with only that idea in mind. Except this time, we ended in disaster. Neither of the guys could perform and neither of us girls enjoyed the situation. The next morning all four of us decided to stop our sexual exercises and stay just ordinary vanilla friends as we were before. However, our agreement did not work out. I mean, it worked for not having sex, but, unfortunately, not for re-building our friendship.

We still communicate with Alden and Millry and still meet sometimes (just a couple of times a year). Yet, we've lost interest in our close friendship.

Involving vanilla friends in sexual activities is another common mistake of Lifestyle beginners. They are either thinking it is the shortest and less complicated way leading to sex, or they are afraid of the process of looking for strangers.

No matter how determined you are to become swingers, never try to seduce your vanilla friends. If you wish (and are sure you would be understood in the right way), you could talk to them about your Lifestyle activities. You could introduce them to the Lifestyle; even bring them to some party if they want to go. Just never, ever play with them!

As our experiences and many similar experiences of our Lifestyle friends demonstrate, the most likely outcome is that you will fracture your friendship.

Frankly, many of our vanilla friends know what we are doing. Some, because of us, have started swinging, too. One couple of our best vanilla friends (do you remember Alan, our starting point Lifestyle adviser?) were swinging even before we started. Sometimes, we meet Alan and his wife at swing parties and have some fun together. However, we never had sex with them. We never will.

During our years in the Lifestyle, we realized that establishing a vanilla friendship is more difficult than a swinging one. So, keep your vertical and horizontal friends separate.

Full swap or soft swap?
By Larry and Mia

Your comfort is all that matters.

The level of your participation in swinging is your own decision.

Soft swap gives you the possibility to experience sexual contact with others without the feeling of deep involvement. If you have an inconsistency between your sexual desires and a somewhat inhibited state of mind, soft swap could settle it. Many swingers start with the soft swap as a temporary compromising stage in their Lifestyle path. Many of them continue further down the road (or should we say "up the road"?) to full swap. At the same time, many feel comfortable at this stage and practice soft-swap only.

Full-swappers usually do not interact with "softies." Furthermore, some of them label soft-swappers as non-serious people. Some even think they are not swingers at all. But everything in the Lifestyle that brings fun and feels good *is swinging*.

Personally, we are not into soft play. It is not enough for us. Nevertheless, we accept anyone's right to practice soft swap as the only swinging activity. Furthermore, we have several friends in the Lifestyle who are softies. See, it is not necessary to play with others to become friends in the Lifestyle. Sharing swinging beliefs and values is enough reason for this friendship just by itself.

It is somewhat frustrating for swingers like us to give up on people we would love to play with just because they are not into full swap. Therefore, if you are full-swappers, protect yourselves from disappointment and misuse of your fun time by avoiding events that attract mostly curious people, watchers, and softies.

Another (much smaller) group of swinging couples are swingers who locate themselves between soft and full swaps. Those are so-called *partially full-swappers*. Half of such a couple is up to intercourse with strangers while the other half is not. Usually, men are more unrestrained.

We have friends, Mendel and Leda, who are a long-time soft-swap couple. Soft swap suits Leda, but Mendel has never given up his hope to convert her into full swap. They arrived at a give-and-take solution. Leda allows her husband to have intercourse with other women but stays "soft" herself.

Finding another couple who would agree to play with them in ordinary two-on-two situations may be complicated, but they are busy enough on the club scene. Mendel is a great lover with a perfect tool, and some ladies come to clubs hoping to find a partner of his caliber. Husbands respect their wives' fantasy and help them make it a reality. As for Leda, she enjoys watching Mendel in action and is always nearby. They have found their own way of swinging.

Same room or separate rooms?
By Larry

> *The ability to enjoy your sex life is central.*
> *I don't give a shit about anything else.*
> —Dudley Moore

Some swingers' ads and Internet profiles explicitly read, "We are a *same-room* couple." What's this about? What makes sex in the same or separate rooms different? This is all about watching (or not) your loved one while he/she is having sex, and, at the same time, about your partner watching you.

First, being able to observe your partner playing translates into being secure. You feel yourself in full control of the situation and are not afraid something weird might happen. (Remember, you are having sex with strangers.)

Second, this way you make sure both of you are comfortable enough in that action.

Third, you upgrade your confidence in each other and cultivate mutual trust.

Finally, yet importantly, you are capable of enjoying your partner's activities in addition to your own, which adds to the fun for most swingers.

A separate room play introduces a new level of sensation you might want to experience at some point. It is, in fact, a short-term splitting of your relationship for you to feel yourselves as a sexually independent man and woman. It could provide you with a capacity of being your true selves and might fulfill some exceptionally personal sexual fantasies.

Should you pursue same-room rule or should you separate for both of you to have more fun? Your own vision is the right choice. If you are beginners, you should start from same-room play because it would help you to stay confident. I would not recommend separate-room play to couples whose mutual trust is not absolute, regardless of their swinging experience. Your relationship must be free from jealousy if you try separate rooms. Also, keep in mind that separate play is only safe with people you know well and fully trust.

Our first experience relating to separate swinging goes back to our vacation at Hedo a few years ago. We already checked out on the last day of our stay, and the bellboy had picked up our suitcases. We were spending our final hours at the nude pool. We mingled with our long-time single friend Alex at the swim-up bar when I suggested a little farewell threesome. Mia reminded me, "We gave up our room already and have no place to play." Alex offered his room instead. Mia was not enthusiastic, though.

Suddenly, I had an idea. I never realized it was growing inside of me. I asked, "Mia, why don't you go to Alex's room, just the two of you? I will wait for you here." Mia looked a little puzzled. We didn't have this item in our repertoire before. We had always played together. Nevertheless, even before she answered, I noticed a blaze in her eyes that, I knew, was a sure sign of desire. She asked, "Honey, are you sure you want me to do it?" I confirmed. We agreed they would return to the bar in exactly one hour, and they left.

Frankly, that was one of the toughest hours of my life. I had neither any jealous feelings for Mia nor doubts about Alex behaving appropriately. We knew him for a couple of years and had played together multiple times and on different scenes. Still, it was an unusual situation for me, and I started to have some regrets.

I was relieved when they came back in one hour. First I noticed a wide happy smile on Mia's face. I knew her happiness was my own achievement; all my worries were gone, too. The second we met, Mia expressed her gratefulness for me being so considerate and trusting, and we had sex right away, right on the beach. That was one of the best and most memorable experiences of our lives.

Some time after, Mia told me she would always remember this episode just because it was a cherry on the top of the whole vacation. As we realized then, we could do whatever each of us wishes to do and, no matter what, we would stay together forever and dedicate the rest of our lives to each other. The last tiniest doubts were gone. We truly revived our vows.

We've done many "separate rooms" since. Still, we prefer same-room play. We do not establish our preference on any trust-related issues. We are well past the period when we had any fears about our ability to keep sex separate from love. It is rather because we both enjoy watching each other in action. We do find something special in separate room play, but for us it is like missing half the fun if we do not share our excitement visually.

Tweaking the age

By Larry and Mia

A pragmatic approach is always a champion.

Age defines your appropriate spot in the Lifestyle. In fact, any matching between couples starts here, and it's all about people's priorities. Some would accept a wide age range for their contacts, some prefer people younger, and some only date older people.

The only option to learn about people's age before you meet them is to consider their own statement on the matter. Yet, keep in mind, potentials here can be different.

We think, the only ones honest about their age groups are those from their 20s to early 30s and those in their 70s. Both these groups don't have to worry that disclosing their actual age could affect their attractiveness and sexual performance. Hence, they are not motivated to be untruthful.

Being in the age range from 30 to 40, people could make some minor corrections, only if they believe they appear younger than they really are.

After 40, many of us start to experience an obvious temptation to declare ourselves younger, at least on the first date. This is where we start making *real* alterations to our age, and the older our age is, the braver these tweaks are.

True, no one expects you to provide your exact age. Yet, if you are up to making some adjustments, please be realistic. Do not try to make fools out of your dates or (most importantly) out of yourselves. Do not tell them you turn 45 next year if you look 55.

If you are fearless enough to verbally position yourselves into a younger age group, please be prepared to do everything in your power to achieve a physical condition and an attitude that are consistent with your pronouncement. Work out, watch your style, take modern dance lessons, and be on top of any conversation.

If you wish to appear younger and more active, be younger and more active!

Women rule the Lifestyle
By Mia

> A woman with one lover is an angel, a woman with two lovers is a monster, but a woman with three lovers is a woman.
> —Victor Hugo

> There are two kinds of women, those who want power in the world and those who want power in bed.
> —Jackie Onassis

> Women need a reason to have sex. Men just need a place.
> —Billy Crystal

Imagine the following situation: Two couples meet. After a little mingling, the men come to an agreement, and all four happily have sex. Does this scene seem real? Something tells me most of you would not believe it does.

Now a different picture: after a little mingling, the women come to that agreement and all four happily have sex. What do you think about this one? It sounds more reasonable, doesn't it?

So, why are two the above similar scenarios so different in the end? Because *women rule the Lifestyle*. Nothing could happen in swinging without ladies' curiosity and final approval.

Men and women react differently in similar situations. For instance, studies show that women first notice bodies and men notice faces when meeting new people of the opposite gender.

Furthermore, for sexual choices, we women are more emotional and spirit-motivated. Our men, as a rule, do not require that somewhat complex internal analysis when making their choice of sexual partner. Men are easy. If they see someone attractive enough, it translates for them into an immediate strong desire of having sex with that person. It may be true that "Man thinks with his penis."

Regardless, the ladies always start the fun in the Lifestyle. They define how this fun should happen and how long it should continue. Even more, we women can easily stop it right in the middle if something goes wrong from our perspective. Because in the Lifestyle, woman is *master* while man is *servant!*

Realize and use this conclusion in your everyday swinging practice. No matter what event you are visiting, a meet-and-greet, club, or private party, if you spotted a couple you would like to get closer to, your better half should perform all the preliminary actions leading to your common fun. She should approach the couple and start all the talking. She is the only person who is able to reach a play agreement, and first with that couple's lady. If ladies do not like each other, nothing will ever happen between you four.

Our friends, Dirk and Lisa, have approached the above rule in an interesting way. Dirk once said, "Two of us make a Lifestyle couple, and Lisa is the PR person for this couple."

Chapter 4

The Lifestyle vs. Vanilla

Who are those swingers anyway?
By Mia

> *When the sun comes up, I have morals again.*
> —Elizabeth Taylor

They don't look happy. They are most definitely not swingers.

People come to the Lifestyle from all walks of life and every line of duty. You'll find as many rich people as working-class ones, as many white collars as blue collars. Every occupation has its representatives here—from teachers to police officers and military, from doctors and attorneys to truck drivers.

Expect all ages, from early 20s to late 70s and even older (once we met a couple whose husband was 84). Every nationality, race, creed, and religion is present as well. (One of our friends, religious Catholics, told us that even before they started swinging they were searching the *Bible* and did not find in it anything that restricts swinging or treats it as a sin of any kind. Let's consider it as their personal finding, though.)

Based on what you already know, you may decide that the swingers are not irregular and weird people, and you would be right. We are normal in "real" life since we have no choice but to blend into the social environment. We have to be just those people next door for everyone around. Still, something makes swingers a bit "off the row."

Once, at some vanilla party (mostly couples from their 40s to their 50s), one of the guests asked us how we managed to keep our relationship in such great shape. We asked in return, "Why do you think it is?" The man answered, "Folks, you two look like you've just been married!" True, we did not realize until then how unusual our behavior could appear to vanilla people. For us, it was natural to hug and kiss each other's cheeks from time to time and smile to each other. We did not intend for it to have any sexual meaning. We simply did not care to keep our signs of love from popping up. Evidently, others noticed the difference.

At our Lifestyle get-togethers, we behave without even trying to control our feelings and emotions. We become our true selves, which is so natural and feels as good as being naked on a beach. As a result, some of it affects our normal-life behavior (unintentionally, of course). Yes, we are trying to control ourselves outside the swinging world, but others still seem to spot some unusual signs.

While making their first steps, Lifestyle newbies are often amazed that swingers are such open, warm, and inviting people. Exceptions exist, but, yes, most of us are.

We fondly look back on our first time at Hedo. We were surprised with the atmosphere we had never experienced before. We found no separate groups of people on the beach: groups playing cards, groups reading books, etc. Instead, people shaped one large crowd where everyone was smiling at one another. Nobody cared who we were and how much money we made, how big our house was, and how expensive our car was. People were naked and equal, therefore, completely open, laid-back, and friendly. They accepted us right away.

Being able to compare vanilla and Lifestyle people for years, we have concluded the average swinging person is happier and friendlier than the average vanilla one.

Sexual fulfillment leads to a different state of both mind and body by enhancing several vital processes. It also improves the mood. We swingers are often happy without any reason. Even our real problems seem to be not that significant.

If you see a couple smiling and looking at each other with love and passion, if their behavior shouts they are comfortable and happy with each other, they might be swingers.

Sometimes, being in a vanilla crowd, we pick up glances we know right away come from Lifestyle people. We just feel it!

Are you attractive?
By Mia

> *Appearance isn't about looking good, It's about feeling good.*
> —Bill Strong

The vanilla mentality presents us swingers with one more misconception: only attractiveness matters. Many Lifestyle newcomers have doubts about their looks—and how their looks would affect the odds of attracting other people.

Attractiveness is subjective. Your appearance alone, while important, will not be the only factor affecting anyone's decision. Many things affect it. Appearance is just one aspect. For some people, it would be more important and for some less.

Even if we assume a perfectly looking Ken & Barbie couple exists in the real world (and they happen to be swingers), they would definitely have some issues beyond their outer shell. From our experience, the better people look, the more self-centered and egotistic they may be. They sometimes think they are performing an act of benevolence just by talking to others. We don't need any favors in swinging and prefer equal situations. The majority of swingers are regular girl/guy next-door kind of people with all the usual look-and-feel attributes.

No one is perfect, including you. The question is: are you good *enough?* Our first time at Hedo gave us a great illustration on the subject. Many people there weren't easy on the eyes. We would never agree playing with them (at least at the time), but all of them were *busy.* Everyone managed to find playmates in the end.

During our time in the Lifestyle, we never met any couple rejected at all times and by everyone. In most cases, there is someone around who is a reasonable match.

Never underestimate your appearance, though. It's complicated, if possible at all, to change the shape of your bodies and make your faces beautiful if you think they are not. At the same time, it's up to you to present yourselves in the best possible light. A big Lifestyle *must* is to dress properly and to keep yourselves well groomed and hygienically clean.

First, remove excessive hair from private areas. We are not living in the '70s anymore. Most swingers prefer shaved or neatly trimmed genitalia. (We once had a club experience where no one wanted to play with an attractive guy just because of his excessive pubic hair.) Don't forget your armpits, too! Trim ear and nose hair. Spruce your eyebrows. Make sure your mustache and beard, if any, are in the best shape. Use a young fragrance, but just a hint. Some people are allergic to scents, and for some too much aroma is a huge turnoff.

Always take a long shower right before leaving for a party. Make sure your bodies are clean. Once at our own party, an attractive enough gentleman had such bad body odor it was nearly impossible to survive near him. As a result, he and his wife had no success at the party and we didn't invite them again.

Another reminder: make sure you trim and file your fingernails and toenails.

Finally, pay attention to your clothing. Your clothes are nothing less than the way you present your initial swinging statement. Dress to look younger, to impress. Be positively sure that it is never possible to over-dress (or should I say "under-dress"?) in the Lifestyle. You don't want to look casual at swinging events. Swinging is not casual by itself and punishes those who think it is!

All these pointers would help you to feel confident, which translates into your success in the Lifestyle. Yes, appearance is important, since it gives a first impression about you. Yet, it is not self-sufficient, because:

Confidence, attitude, and chemistry are the keys

By Larry

Ugly, but confident!

We were preparing to leave for a party. As with most men, I was dressed and ready to go earlier than Mia was. I asked, "So, honey, how do I look?" She looked me over and smiled, "As usual, you are fat, ugly, but confident!"

Well, I am somewhat overweight, yet handsome rather than ugly. However, Mia's answer perfectly plays up the subject of this section—self-confidence and the right attitude are far more important than appearance.

Imagine the situation that can often be seen at clubs or private parties. The first couple is young and attractive but quietly sits in a dark corner, gently smiling and waiting for something to happen. The second couple might not be as young and attractive but is more active and full of life. They chat with others, dance, and make every possible step to get in touch with as many people around them as possible. No doubt, the second couple will have more fun at the final party stage.

Confidence and an active mindset are the most important factors defining your odds of becoming sexually attractive to other swingers. You need a decent appearance, an ability to hold an intelligent conversation, and a good sense of humor to make that *click* happen.

Sexual chemistry matters, too. Unfortunately, you cannot do much about it. Either you feel desire for someone or you don't, and vice versa. Therefore, you will never get everyone you like, yet you will be able to attract more than enough people to have fun.

Emanuel and Angie, an inexperienced Lifestyle couple, once came to one of our house parties. An attractive duo in their 20s, they were tense and shy from the beginning, did not talk much with others, and did not react to our attempts to make them feel at ease. When it came to play time, I noticed them playing with each other. I came closer to them with that old swingers' joke, "You know, at swing parties it's a bad luck to play with the person you came with! You're losing points!"

I did not expect them to take the joke seriously. They did, though. They ended their play immediately and just stood in the corner watching others in action. Some gentlemen approached Angie. No ladies approached Emanuel because they all were busy. Since our parties are orgies, we do not play couple-to-couple. We informed Emanuel and Angie of that in advance and they confirmed that this setting was okay with both of them. Apparently, they were not ready and were, to say the least, frustrated. I tried to teach them on-the-fly how to act properly. Yet, it did not work for them and, as a result, they left early. We never heard from them again.

The wrong attitude and lack of self-confidence may lead to failure and frustration in the Lifestyle.

Are swingers aggressive?
By Larry and Mia

To thine ends, set bashfulness aside.
Who fears to ask, to be denied.
—Thomas Herrick

Unfortunately, far from every swinging couple has an active attitude. At the same time, dynamic people are the most successful in the Lifestyle. More than that, the Lifestyle itself exists only because of them. Someone has to approach first for fun to happen.

Let's try to answer the question contained in the title of this section based on what you already know at this point. Yes, you could say that well-determined and self-confident swingers are aggressive. However, they also possess an understanding of swinging aggressiveness, or else they would not be successful at all.

To be aggressive in the Lifestyle does not mean to be hostile, violent, or pushy. Instead, it means being self-assured, energetic, and not at all anxious. It also means being not afraid to ask others, not frightened of offering yourselves while staying open-minded, welcoming, and friendly to everyone around.

We can only talk here about up-to-a-certain-extent aggressiveness. As a rule, aggressive swingers know all the applicable limits. They will greet you, they will mingle with you, and they will ask you to play with them. Up to this point, they will be firm and motivated.

Yet, if you let them know you'd rather decline their offer, they will never insist and will never follow you throughout the night hoping you will change your mind. Instead, they will stay pleasant and open to you and will never have any hard feelings.

Do you know why? Because they are *aggressive!* It is not a big deal for them to move on. Thanks to their attitude, they will find their fun anyway, and they know that. They have substantial experience proving this fact.

As you can see, aggressiveness in swinging has a different meaning compared with the vanilla world. You'll find many terminological mismatches on your journey to the Lifestyle. Vanilla logic does not always apply to the Lifestyle and vice versa.

Age and swing
By Larry and Mia

> *For the young man is handsome, but the old man is great.*
> —*Victor Hugo*

> *Sex can be fun after eighty, after ninety, and after lunch!*
> —*George Burns*

What age is the best to start swinging? There are no hard rules and recommendations; it is subjective and individual. Many situations move people into the Lifestyle. Here are just a few examples:

- A young man receives as a gift a week at Hedo. It can be a present for birthday, graduation, etc. Then, the Lifestyle opens its doors for him as early as age 20 to 25.
- Young couples are looking for satisfaction of their sexual fantasies right after their wedding (or even before). They could become swingers at the age range from 20 to 35.
- Well-established married couples with children who don't require thorough attention anymore spot breaches in the intimate part of their relationship and try to find ways to enhance it. They are in their mid-30s to their 50s.
- People like the authors of this book who engage in swinging as soon as they first find out about its existence and feel nothing prevents them from taking their part in it. It can happen anywhere from their 20s to their 60s.

All that is important is your personal, mutual, and unambiguous approval of your life-turning choice, not when it occurs. The best proof of this decision being right would be regretting that your swinging activities did not start even earlier than they did—a common feeling among swingers.

The Lifestyle has no age limitations besides a legal one: you should be over 18 to take your part. If you require proof, go to a swing club, visit swing conventions, or travel to a Lifestyle-friendly resort. At these places, you will see all ages represented. For instance, couples in their 20s and in their 70s are not rare at Hedo, while the largest part of people there are in the 35 to 50 age range.

Attending Lifestyle conventions as well as vacationing at Lifestyle resorts always allows you to blend with any age group, whichever you feel you belong to, whichever suits you best, and whichever you can fit in.

Do you remember the starting question of this book? Here it comes again. "Would you be interested in having sex with someone twice your age or someone twice as young?" The authors had not had a chance to play with twice-older persons. We did not manage to meet any Lifestyle people in their 90s so far! There are not many of them around. However, we have many friends in their 20s as members of our playgroup. Once, at our party, someone asked us, pointing to one of our guests, a 22-year-old stud, "Is this your son?" Our answer was, "No, this is Mia's boy toy. Our son is older!"

We play with much younger couples and singles. For them, it means they are having encounters with people twice their age. Many young swingers are looking for experienced Lifestyle contacts because they prefer the real no-drama situations to inexperience, selfishness, egocentricity, and, thus, an uncertain outcome. They would like to learn from older like-minded people. Mature swingers have a lot to share. Besides, they have a wide range of Lifestyle connections and possess information and experiences worth acquiring.

That said, before you attend a Lifestyle event, find out the average age of the people expected to be there. If the crowd is too old for you, you might not be interested in the party. Chances are you will find yourselves leaving for home earlier than expected. And vice versa, if the group is too young, you could feel uncomfortable, and the odds of finding playmates for the night would not be promising. Anything is possible though.

What do swingers talk about?
By Mia

Here comes yet another part of the excitement.

Being in the Lifestyle affects our behavior a lot. Thanks to our way of life and free mindset, at our events we swingers have an opportunity to be *truly us*. Our unique philosophy influences the whole atmosphere of our gatherings.

From the first time you are at a swing party or in a swing club, you will sense how different these gatherings are when compared with their vanilla counterparts. These differences manifest themselves first in swingers' conversations.

So, what do we talk about at our get-togethers? Let me begin with what we *do not* talk about. We do not discuss:

- Politics.
- Economy.
- Children.
- Work.
- Age and age-related as well as health and health-related issues.
- Diets and dieting.

Some of the above topics could be lightly touched, but just at the initial party stage. Yet, the subject never gets supported and continued because it is not what you would like to talk about while staring at the promising smile of an enticing lady next to you, or while you are looking at an attractive gentleman whose eyes tell you what he really thinks about.

If we swingers meet someone we have never met before, we usually exchange our names (just *first* names, never ask for last ones) and tell each other where we live (again, just an area, not an address). At this first acquaintance point, the following questions are typical:

- How did you learn about this party (club, resort, convention, etc.)?
- Who referred/invited you here?
- Who are you already familiar with here?
- How long have you been in the Lifestyle?
- What are your swinging interests?
- How did you get into swinging?
- What are your favorite swing clubs (resorts, conventions, etc.)?

After we ask all these questions and acknowledge all the answers, the next logical step is to search for common friends: "Do you know that couple, A and B? No? What about C and D then? Yes, they are, they are...Wait a second! We've met them just last week at the club, and they told us about their new friends E and F. Are you these E and F? Are you? This is unbelievable! What a small world! Nice meeting you guys!"

If we, instead, talk to our old friends or someone already familiar, we might be focusing on something different. Of course, multiple variations to the following will exist, depending on the place and the party theme.

Matters we chat about are different at each of the party segments. At first, the *mingling* part of the party:

- Latest movies with a complete analysis of actors' body parts.
- Fresh rumors and gossip, normally funny ones that do not provoke cruel debates.
- Sports, with obligatory discussions about sportsmen's looks and their possible sexual qualities.
- Sexually oriented travel experiences: Lifestyle resorts, swing clubs in Europe, Amsterdam's Red Light District, etc.
- Clubs and parties experiences: quality, rules, recommendations.
- Latest swinging developments: new friends. Yes, we share this information, and don't be surprised if someone contacts you by your other friends' referral. Still, it could happen only if you have a Web profile at a swingers' site! Nobody will ever expose your direct e-mail address as well as share your phone number.

At the *naked* party stage:

- Tattoos.
- Body piercing.
- Suntan and tan lines.
- Witty hairstyles of genitalia areas with compliments to their owners.
- Degree of endowment (more compliments).
- Exchanges of just-happened experiences. Recommendations to use your chance immediately. "Guys, see that couple in the left corner? They are really wild! You must try them right away or you'll be sorry!"

Usually, at the *naked* point of the party, expect a second round of name exchanges with new people. Yes, you already asked their names before, but just on a reason of supporting a conversation, and you could easily forget them. This time, you need to memorize these names (along with obtaining their e-mail address) because you will probably want to meet these people again, provided you enjoyed your sexual encounter with them.

When we are leaving for home, we always say goodbye. Unlike some vanilla counterparts, the majority of swingers are polite and friendly people and it would be simply improper to leave without it.

Swinging is a show!
By Mia

The most important thing in acting is to be able to laugh and cry.
If I have to cry, I think of my sex life.
If I have to laugh, I think of my sex life.
—Glenda Jackson

Don't try to reach Broadway, just do it your way...

The time we swingers devote to our Lifestyle activities is our *free* time, free from work, children, and other vanilla obligations. We value this time and would like to fill it with happiness and bliss to the fullest. During these moments, we expect to feel completely separated from our routines and troubles. We are eager to position ourselves in the middle of positive emotions and replenish our bodies and minds with upbeat energy and happiness. We like to tell and hear jokes and funny tales. We love to make chivalrous compliments and accept the same in return.

Swingers create a unique environment (quite different from the vanilla one) for themselves. Some of them realize this fact, some don't, but they all play their *roles* on the stage of the Lifestyle Theater.

Yes, swinging is a show, and Lifestyle people are the actors. The only difference from a real show is we swingers play *ourselves*. We play happy, pleased with our lives, open for new contacts and experiences, and issues-free selves.

It even looks and feels a little theatrical. Others closely watch us just as they watch real actors, trying to evaluate our performance. Each time we leave for some party, we feel somewhat similar to entering a concert stage widely open to immeasurable space full of a fussy audience.

Besides being perfectly groomed and tastefully dressed, you should exhibit an appropriate behavior, an open smile, and self-confidence to play your role effectively. If you do not possess those qualities as a part of your vanilla personality, *play* them while you present your swinging one. Play, you won't regret it!

Depending on your acting abilities and skills and on your willingness to perform, your participation in the show could be one of the following:

1. **Passive.** Simply put, you watch what is going on around you. Yet you must show your openness, true curiosity, and deliberate concern, as well as your *a priori* approval, your true internal joy, and positive attitude to everyone around. Most important, you have to look happy and free of any worries. Besides, you should be ready to support the actual show stars in every way possible.
2. **Active.** Intermingling with old friends, getting to know new people, dancing, singing, playing musical instruments, performing striptease, i.e. doing everything you can for everyone around to feel relaxed and happy.
3. **Combination** of (1) and (2).

While roles (2) and (3) above are preferable, role (1) is mandatory! Otherwise, you won't blend into the environment. If you were unable to play role (1), you would definitely be out of the show loop. Therefore, you would reduce your chances to succeed to somewhat of a problematical level.

Once, at some Hedo group party on one of the last days of our stay, an attractive young single guy approached me and asked why I didn't show any interest in him during the whole week. He told me, all this time he was trying to attract my attention making circles around me at the pool and on the beach. Yet he was too shy to initiate contact himself. He was watching my easiness in making new friends and talking to people and was wondering why I avoided him. My answer was, "Of course, I've seen you around, and my husband even pointed to you. However, you looked as if you were unhappy and troubled. You never smiled, and I don't want to deal with this kind of attitude while on vacation. This was not what I needed. I was looking (and am still looking!) for unrestrained people, happy faces, easiness, and positive energy!"

We finally got closer and even played with the gentleman. Both of us enjoyed it. Yet it happened only because the hosts of that party invited him. Otherwise, he would have never gotten my interest.

Please keep in mind, if you are not exactly this happy smiling person everyone around likes to be with, play this version of yourself! Play, you won't regret it!

We were friends with George and Elizabeth for several months when George admitted he was afraid to talk to me at their first meeting with us because he did not know what kind of reaction he could expect from Larry. George told me, "When we first met, Larry did not smile much. Others usually respect people of his height and build. So, I did not feel like I was ready to experiment with his temper. I was frightened to tell an extra joke and make an extra compliment to you. I was wondering what will happen to me if Larry's neutral face expression would suddenly change to anger! I was afraid he could punch me! Well, now I know your husband is a kind, intelligent, open, and cordial person. But who could imagine he had all these qualities by the way he looked then?"

George's tale was a good lesson for us. Larry's demeanor has changed since then. My husband has discovered a gifted actor inside himself, and his efforts produced an instant result.

Analyze your behavior by trying to look at yourself from the other's perspective. You are okay if people wish to approach you and spend some time in your company; otherwise, something is wrong with you. Rehearse until you achieve the appropriate outcome. Forget about your shyness and nervousness. Let all your good inner qualities shine through your outer shell. Share them with everyone around, and you will reward yourself. Who cares if you play it or if this is your natural self? It does not matter! What matters is the swingers' strong determination of having fun and exchanging positive energy and pleasurable emotions.

Play, you won't regret it!

Chapter 5

Meeting on the Internet

Swing websites
By Larry and Mia

You can do it in one single click!

If you seriously intend to get involved in the Lifestyle, consider membership in at least one swing website as a necessity. The Internet can provide you with a wealth of information, and swinging is no exception. We got the majority of our Lifestyle contacts from this very source.

Quite a few websites cater to swingers. Some already have an established reputation; others have just started. We don't provide any site names here, but to find them, make a Web search for "swing," "swingers," "swinging," "Lifestyle," or any combination of those for many useful links.

You would not want to use every website, though. Your first priority should be finding local people and learning about local activities and events. Therefore, consider a given website's popularity in your area as your key criteria. The more members from your geographic region a particular website accommodates, the more beneficial your membership would be.

Some websites have a free trial period; others have permanent free accounts. If you are a trial or free member, you are having several restrictions you could avoid by obtaining a paid membership instead. Our tip is to try the given site for some time free. Decide on becoming a paid member based on the results of your evaluation.

A single month membership could cost from $10 to $20. If you prefer paying for the whole year, the same month would cost more than twice cheaper. Some sites have lifetime memberships. By paying what amounts to two or three years' membership, you could become a member forever, until you are no longer interested or the site is out of business (whichever comes first).

In addition to giving a means of contacting other members through its internal e-mail system and internal IM, a Lifestyle website may present you with many additional features. It can have a chat room, forums, and discussion areas. It can provide local, national, and worldwide information on swing clubs. It can advertise private parties, adult resorts, and swing conventions. In addition, it can offer an array of commercial links to online sex shops and sex boutiques. Some sites have areas for exchanging sex stories, real experiences, and so on.

Your profile on a swing website
By Larry

Marketing the right way is important.

Establishing your profile on a website is not complicated. Just answer questions about your location, age, swinging preferences, etc. Each of your answers will constitute a search parameter for other members who may try to connect with you. These same filters will also help you obtain a list of profiles you might be interested in contacting. Some sites will ask more questions, some less.

If you choose to, you will be able to set your profile defaults to block a certain type of the site members from contacting you, such as single men, single women, couples, trial or free members, members without posted pictures, uncertified members, and so on. These options differ from site to site.

You should complete a main part of your profile that is nothing more than descriptive answers to general matters such as "What are you looking for?," "Describe yourself," "Your experience," "Your sexual fantasies," and so on.

The site will provide you with an option of creating a profile title. Make it a short sentence reflecting the spirit of your profile.

Every bit of information you supply is subject to change at any time. You can modify anything, including your location and gender. For example, you can easily change a couple's profile into the single's one and vice versa.

Make your profile as truthful as possible and accommodate all your priorities, desires, requirements, and policies. Incompatible members may still contact you (some people do not read profiles), yet many fewer than otherwise.

Any website will allow you to upload pictures as a part of the profile. Some of them will be open to every member (public pictures). The others (private or personal) will be accessible to only members who you authorize to view them. Some websites let you create multiple galleries and personalize access to them. Placing at least several public pictures on your profile greatly improves your rating. People view profiles with pictures about 15 times more often compared with profiles without them (a statistic from one of the websites the authors are members of). Some members won't consider you serious if your profile has no pictures; others will even block you from contacting them.

An important feature of virtually every website is *validations* (*certifications* on other sites). Other members can validate you, as well as you can certify them. These validations always add more weight to your initial profile's content. While you compile and present your profile *yourselves*, *others* certify you. Their words can tell a lot about you. As a rule, a website would not allow you to change the text of the validation, but you can decline it in whole and, therefore, avoid attaching it to your profile.

Below are some of the important features and parameters of a profile in more detail.

Location

No websites are interested in your real address. All they ask for is your ZIP code. It makes a perfect sense to supply a correct code, or at least the area that is close enough to yours. This way you will be able to view profiles of your closest neighbors at the top of the list while making a search or checking out who is online.

An additional benefit of sorting profiles by their locality is that, by changing your location, you would be able to move (virtually) to any desired geographic region. Let's say, you are intending to visit a place for vacation or business and would like to check out local swingers. All you need to do is to update the location of your profile with the ZIP code of the area in question and make a new search. The first profiles on your list will be profiles of people residing there.

Age

You won't gain anything by being untruthful about your age. You could cut a few years based on your own look-and-feel situation, but be realistic to save yourselves from the frustration of denial by potential dates.

Height/Weight

Taking off a few pounds might work. However, keep in mind if your real weight is 180 pounds while you indicate it as just 140 pounds, you still weigh 180. So, be reasonably honest with this number as well.

Swinging preferences

Different websites use different terminology here. Even so, this question is all about how you situate yourselves in swinging, about what you are looking for: tame pleasures, soft swap, full swap, etc. Be specific and honest.

Profile title

When site members perform a search, they only see a list of profile titles and default pictures. All other information will be available after (and if) they open your profile. So make them open it. Reveal your fantasy and create a small teaser phrase that characterizes you best and differentiates you from others. It can be anything from just "Looking for fun" to "Is anyone up for the hot tub tonight?", "Let's welcome spring with gang bang!," or "Emergency service is available."

Pictures

Uploading pictures on your profile is a huge plus. Unless you are overly discreet, I would advise you to use this feature. To tell you the truth, we were concerned, too, and initially did not attach any pictures to our profile, but the number of responses was so low, we decided to try it.

If you prefer, you can post public pictures that do not reveal your faces as well as your full bodies. Yet, show your creativity and make sure they attract attention anyway. Our public pictures either are some parts of us or have no heads, which is common for swingers' profiles. On the other hand, some members don't hesitate posting their face pictures, but those are people who do not care about privacy.

Concentrate on pictures of your better half, maybe even her pictures only. According to some websites' statistics, more than 80% of your profile *initial* viewers are men of the couples and single men (if you did not block them).

As for your personal/private pictures, you will decide who should have access to them. You will want to open them to someone you would like to meet. Hence, your personal gallery should include face and full-body shots of both of you.

The main rule about pictures—never send them to an outside e-mail address. All swing websites protect your privacy fully. No one can copy or download your pictures while on the site. However, you can't say where your pictures could end up if you sent them to an outside e-mail address.

Validations

Do others and yourselves a favor by only certifying people you have actually swung with in the past. Remember, it does not matter if members you validate are real people. The only thing that counts is if they are *real swingers*.

Main part of the profile

The other members might find your profile by using age, area, and some other criteria, but they will decide to contact you based on what you say in your profile. This part is also about answering website's questions. You need only be descriptive and imaginative. Think of your answers as your Lifestyle resume. State something to get you noticed, to encourage other people to be interested in you. It must be sincere, yet out of the ordinary, witty, charming, and able to spark interest.

Below are a few sample profiles. Judge yourselves which of them you like, which you find objectionable, and why.

Couple's profile

Just for fun!
We are looking for:
Other couples
Description:
We are fun and open.
Our experience/fantasies:
We'll tell you when we meet.
What do you want to add:
We'll tell you when we meet.

Single man's profile

I am ready for everything
We are looking for:
I am ready for everything.

Description:
I am ready for everything.
Our experience/fantasies:
I am ready for everything.
What do you want to add:
I am ready for everything.

Below are examples of well-written profiles. I have an authorization to use some parts of our friends' profiles, yet none of the following exists on any website as presented here.

Single gentleman's profile
Your intelligence is a big turn on.
We are looking for:
I am interested in encounters with couples and selected single ladies. I am open to everything; yet do not participate in homosexual or bi activity. This is a definite and final "No!"
Description:
I am a highly attractive Caribbean-native with an athletic body, 6'3", 225 lb, cool, and appealing. I worship every likely sexual scenario, no matter what it is: private and individual, or open and intense group session.

My parents blessed me with an extra-ordinary endowment. It depends on the current situation, but do not be surprised if "it" gets up to 12 inches!

I am a good dancer and am a ravenous bookworm with an open mind and tolerant intellect. Oddly enough, I also have an unappeasable stamina and am up to satisfying my sexual partners in every way possible.
Our experience/fantasies:
I have been into swinging for quite awhile and have experienced interesting sexual situations.
What do you want to add:
I enjoy people who are intelligent conversationalists and have

a good sense of humor. Indeed, there is no reason in playing with persons who are not at least witty or unusual. Race does not matter, but beauty and sensuality does!

I'm both sexually and intellectually dominant by nature. Therefore, your strong mind (if any) will definitely win points with me.

The ability to distinguish sex from love is one of the most important items in swinging, and I hope you are able to do so. Contact me if you do!

Single lady's profile

The more, the merrier!

We are looking for:

Group sex is my first priority!

Single women or married ones who play without me needing to play with their male partner are welcome as well.

Single guys, I have more of you than I can handle!

Race and age as well as nationality and religion are not important at all.

I truly believe greed is a good philosophy, but I've learned how to share.

Description:

I am 29 years old, cute, downright adorable once you get to know me. I am a sweet girl, attractive, too.

I have nice ass. At the same time, I am a great conversationalist. It is hard to believe these two qualities exist in the same person, isn't it?

I like all forms of sex. I dare you to think of one I would not like. I have no fetishes; don't care for things involving bodily fluids other than cum. That stuff I like a lot. I can even play with it. This is lots of fun.

I love groups, especially the ones where couples can leave their relationship at the door. Singles' groups are great, too. There is no relationship to leave anywhere, and this is very convenient.

Our experience/fantasies:
Yeah, I like to brag, but I am discreet about it.
What do you want to add:
You're just going to have to write and start asking questions. Yet, if you are under 30, please do not even consider contacting me. I am not your teacher, your coach, or your mother.

Lastly, here is our own profile on one of the sites. It may be long, but it does not leave anything about our interests, requirements, and us personally unaddressed.

Real people may meet us at a swing club

Please, read entire profile and only contact us if you are sure we are what you need! We receive tons of e-mails where people offer us things inconsistent with our policies. Don't waste your time. We are what we are! To make it clear from the beginning, we do not meet new people in places other than clubs or group sessions! No two-on-two first dates!

We are looking for:
Couples who know what they want and do not hesitate to make it a reality. People who could add a little icing on top of a cake we already have.

We strongly prefer CPLs where ladies are bi-sexual or at least comfortable with women foreplay.

We respect all the boundaries and accept anyone's right to practice soft swap. More than that, we have many friends in the Lifestyle who are "softies."

Still, we expect you to be a true full swap if you contact us. We are not up to any variation of soft play, including partial partners swap. We hate teasing with no logical continuation. If you consider full swap just as a possibility, but not your primary target, we are not your match.

We do not care much about a "friends first" approach, but always welcome friendship that comes out of sex relations. Several of our partners became close friends, and we meet them on a regular basis. We always welcome out-of-bed fun and laughs, but sorry, we won't take you to a movie or invite for a BBQ. We are here for great sex with no strings attached.

Description:

We are highly educated, intelligent professionals, upscale, happily married, and in love. He is handsome, but somewhat overweight. She is a real beauty with a perfect body. We are truly in the Lifestyle, absolutely in love with Hedo, getting there one or two times a year. We visited several Lifestyle conventions in the past and intend to continue these activities.

We often attend private swing parties as well as host at our place. We visit local swing clubs where we set up our first dates. We manage our active group of swinging friends where we only accept new people by referral of our existing playmates. We are fun, entertaining, easy going, DD free, discreet full-swap same-room CPL.

One more thing to mention: we are honest and polite. If you e-mail us, we always e-mail you back. If we do not feel we are a match for you, we still send you our thanks. We never understood people who are bad mannered enough to not answer at all. We keep track of those persons and, if you are one of them, you can be sure we have no interest in you anymore.

Our experience/fantasies:

We do not memorize our encounters; we just enjoy them. Since we consider ourselves no-drama seasoned swingers, our experience is rather on the extensive side.

As for fantasies, you'll be surprised: there are some left! Yet, BDSM and Water Sports are definitely not among them.

What do you want to add:

We are always happy to meet new people, which brought us here in the first place.

If you read our profile in whole and feel we are what you need, we are ready to give it a chance. We do not require your pictures at all, only one with your faces to recognize you when we meet. We are selective, but we meet virtually every couple interested in us if we feel their profile is a match.

Something we would like to stress here:

We do not tolerate fakes, flakes, and unreliable people. If you promised something and did not keep your word, you do not exist for us anymore.

Basics:

We are friendly, respectful, and not pushy. However:

If you are not ready for full swap, we are not what you need.

If you need several meetings to get closer, we are not what you need.

If you just want to chat and exchange e-mails and pictures, we are not what you need.

If you have a problem using condoms, we are not what you need.

We have a busy life schedule and do not have time for drama. Get to the point!

First dates:

Yes, we are busy and hate to waste our time. Thus, we only schedule first dates at swing clubs and private swing parties where nobody feels obligated and frustrated if that click we all know about did not happen. In this case, we all are free to move on and could stay just like-minded friends. On the contrary, if all agree, we could start fun right away or set another private date in the nearest future. We like to host at our place and have everything necessary ready.

The minute we like you is the minute we are ready for you.

Pictures:

We do not trust pictures.

Being in the Lifestyle for quite some time, we do not see people as beautiful or ugly, short or tall, skinny or fat. For us, you would be *sexually* or *non-sexually* attractive. The only possibility to match is to meet you, talk to you, look into your eyes, and feel your chemistry.

Our personal and private pictures are here for our convenience, but not for public viewing. Normally, we only send our face picture to people we agree to meet with. If you wish to see all our privates, open yours first and be prepared to call us for voice verification, let our ladies talk first.

We do not send our photos outside this website!

Certifications:

We believe certifications are the most important part of any profile. We only accept certs from people we've been intimate with and only certify on this same condition. We do meet with people who are not yet certified.

Here is the last thought to add:

Some of you may not find enough sweet words in this profile, and you know why?

We hate fakes and flakes. They are not any better than thieves. They are stealing your time. They e-mail you, chat with you, and disappear when it comes to an actual meeting without any explanation. How many of them are on this site? Our figure is at least 70%. Therefore, we explicitly designed our policies and profile to keep them off.

Nonetheless, we are nice with real, honest, and reliable people. Try us out if you are those!

I hope all these samples will give you a good idea of what you should have in your profile to bring you an appropriate response from the right people while keeping wrong people away.

Update your profile often to stay consistent with your current preferences, requirements, and policies (they could change, couldn't they?).

Finally, to keep your profile fresh and up-to-date and attract more viewers, switch your profile's default pictures and change its title as often as possible. This simple trick attracts more viewers. We do it almost daily.

Communicating on the Web

By Larry

Make your point proficiently.

The best way to communicate is two-way. Someone will contact you eventually, but you have to be active on your side as well. Search for local swingers, check who is online now, view their profiles, and contact them if interested. You can either send internal e-mail or (if they are online) IM them.

Read profiles carefully. You can save others and yourselves a lot of time that way. Always make your decision on contacting people based on their whole profile, not just their pictures. Getting in touch with others only makes sense if you feel you would be compatible, only if your profiles complement each other, at least in general.

If you decided to write, make sure your e-mail is respectful, addresses their requirements, and states your intentions clearly. Always sign your names (even it they're just fake ones!). E-mail with no signature looks discourteous. E-mails such as "We've read your profile," "You are very hot," "Love your outfits," etc., are unacceptable since they do not reveal your thoughtfulness and do not show your intentions. Our answer to these e-mails is always the same, "Thanks." Such communication leads nowhere.

If a couple asks you to open your personal pictures while contacting them and you don't provide such access, chances are high you won't get a reply.

If someone has contacted you, answer immediately. It's a sign of your positive attitude and reliability. If you are not interested, you can write, "Thank you for picking us out of the crowd. Unfortunately, it seems that we are not compatible, at least now. Swing safely, X & Y." If they look attractive to you, but you are not ready to answer before your partner looks at their profile, send them an instant reply anyway expressing your appreciation and promise to contact them as soon as you are ready. Your answer could read, "Thank you for contacting us and your interest. Please allow us some time for my wife to look at your profile. We will get back to you shortly. XOXO, John."

Do not be frustrated if people don't answer. Either they did not like you, or they are not real swingers. Make your notes on them (most websites allow to post notes that will be attached to the given profile and visible to you only) and move on. Not answering is rude, and you would not want to be involved with impolite people in any case, no matter who they are or how good they might look.

Some of you may say, "E-mails are not fully reliable. Hence, it is never possible to be sure the initial e-mail reached the person in question." This concern is not true for internal website mail systems. Here you can see the status of your e-mail, including the date/time of its delivery, opening, and reply. This nice feature excludes wrong conclusions.

Websites also indicate your previous contacts and let you view your e-mail exchange history with every member. If people contact you again after you have indicated you are not interested, never bother to reply. Block them from accessing your profile.

If people promised to write you back and never did, do not contact them a second time. Reliable swingers do not behave this way. You don't want to waste your precious time with undependable people.

If you received a harsh e-mail (it happens sometimes), report this profile to the site administration and block its possessors from accessing you.

Do not engage in long e-mail exchanges. If it lasts for months with no practical result, i.e. date, something is wrong with your contacts.

Don't hesitate to request a phone conversation with people you would like to meet. Giving them your cell phone number would not hurt your privacy at all. If they won't call you (happens more often than otherwise), you would know they are not for real and, therefore, you can save yourselves time and effort by avoiding further worthless e-mails and picture exchanges. Just make sure all four of you are available for that phone tête-à-tête. Girl-to-girl conversation is the best starter and, as a rule, exposes any possible problems with your counterparts instantly.

Fakes and flakes
By Larry and Mia

It is often not exactly what it looks like.

Do not be surprised if you experience a fair amount of mistreated time while online. Many people out there call themselves swingers, but are not even close to being honest and real. Such an impersonation can have different reasons, yet, in the end, all of these people are either fakes or flakes.

Fakes

Couples' and single ladies' profiles often belong to single men. They use pictures of others to camouflage themselves. Sometimes you can tell those pictures are from magazines.

Those gentlemen are looking for dirty talks and trying to force you to grant them access to your private pictures. (We are attempting to be polite by calling them "gentlemen" as opposed to "jerks.") All these actions probably get them aroused and bring them a sexual pleasure. Some masturbate while looking at your pictures, reading your e-mails, and chatting with you. If you are up to providing them with this opportunity, go ahead. The majority of us swingers aren't.

The other group of profiles belongs to real people. They are what they say they are and do not pretend being someone else, with one significant exception—they claim to do things but are not able to. Those people might be just curious about the Lifestyle activities while trying to look like experienced swingers to attract your attention. Their intentions could be not bad at all; still, their imposture makes them plain fakes.

Often just a half of couple (mostly male) contacts you or accepts your contact. He grants you an access to their personal pictures (and those pictures are real), he asks and answers questions for both of them, and he finally (again for both of them) agrees to meet you. Everything looks and sounds normal and legitimate. However, in reality, the better half of this couple has no idea about any of these activities as well as about you. This couple never comes to the date.

Fakes always disappear as soon as you offer to meet.

Flakes

One variation of flakes is people who might intend to meet you, but, for the reason of swinging inexperience or some drama in their relationship, they change their plans at the last moment.

The second (and most significant by their quantity) deviation of flakes are unreliable people. They can be beginners or experienced swingers; it does not matter. What matters is they don't care about anyone around. They promise you anything and forget about their commitment. These people may schedule two dates at the same time to decide which of the two to keep when they are already in their car.

No matter which of the above two groups you are dealing with, the outcome is always the same—flakes do not care to come and never apologize afterward.

From our experience, fakes and flakes hugely outnumber real reliable swingers on every swing website. The right thing to do is to keep them from contacting you and, at the same time, to save yourselves from mistakenly contacting them. Be careful as much as you can.

How to spot a weird profile
By Larry

Do not trust your eyes; always make sure.

Let's say, someone has contacted you or you would like to contact a profile that looks promising. Even before writing the initial or responding e-mail, perform some evaluation to spot fakes and flakes.

Here are the signs people beyond the given profile have some problems:

There are no validations from other site members

The lack of validations is understandable if the profile is freshly open. People did not have a chance to earn certifications yet. On the other hand, if the profile is out there for more than, let's say four to five months, its owners likely prefer to talk about swinging, but are not really involved in it.

Some site members explain absence of validations by their personal effort of being discreet. Sometimes, they explicitly write in their profiles they do not certify others and do not accept certifications. They utilize a nice phrase for that, "We don't kiss and tell."

In one situation, after our almost two-month-long e-mail exchanges with one of those "we-don't-kiss-and-tellers," they, at the last moment, cancelled a scheduled date with us and stopped any further communication. After almost five years of its existence on the website, their profile is still proud of being not certified. We are sure many people have wasted their valuable time with those fakes exactly as it happened to us.

We cannot think of any valid reason why some people would not certify others they swung with and why it would harm their privacy if others validated them. If they are already there, on the site, and their discretion level does not prevent them from claiming to be swingers, why don't they let others confirm they *really* are?

Profile is free

If the given profile is relatively new for the site, it still may be free. Yet, if people are okay with all the restrictions a free membership introduces, if they rather prefer to save on a small fee than to get rid of them, they are probably not serious about swinging. Make note.

Profile has no recent validations

If the couple received their most recent certification a year ago, there is a possibility something is wrong with these people. Maybe one of them has lost interest in Lifestyle activities. Or they had other problems, such as disease or death in the family, separation or divorce (for married couple), or termination of a temporary relationship (for "single-and-single" pseudo couple).

Be aware: in all these cases, you are dealing with just a half of the former swinging couple, most often a man.

Profile is not active

Websites either stamp profiles with the date of their last online session or enable you to see how many days ago members last logged in. If people did not visit the site for a long time, they likely are not serious about swinging. In our experience, active swingers check their mailbox at least every other day. For this reason, we never contact members who did not do so for more than two weeks.

Pictures are too perfect

Perhaps you see clearly *different* people in each of these pictures. Some pictures may look like works of professional photographers while others appear as if they are amateur. What's more, there is no attempt to hide faces. All these signs are a strong indication of a fake profile.

Gender mismatch

If you are reading a couple's profile and spot some "I" rather than "we" in its text, there are reasonable odds to believe the profile's holder is a single man pretending to be a couple. Additionally, in this case the profile never has certifications.

Sometimes, guys do not even try to make you believe they are a couple. They explicitly create a couple's profile rather than a single male's to get access to other couples' profiles.

Chapter 6

Meeting in person

Your Lifestyle business card
By Larry and Mia

This is important to take care of.

Any information presented on a card looks much better than on some piece of paper or a dinner napkin. Besides, a napkin often ends up in the trash container.

You should always have a sufficient amount of cards with you at any Lifestyle event. If you wish, call them *meeting* cards, not *business*. On these personal cards use your contact information you would like to provide.

What information your card should contain?

Necessary:
- First names of both of you.
- Your direct e-mail address.

Optionally:
- Your swing website and your profile name on it.
- Your telephone number (never give your better half's phone number).
- Your photograph. Remember, swingers do not exchange last names! Instead, everyone remembers you by your first ones. Therefore, if you printed your face picture on your card, it would greatly enhance the chance that people know who you are.

Don't pay full price for these cards. Several websites offer free cards while charging shipping and handling fee only.

Some swing websites provide you with a capability of printing meeting cards. You can customize the card as well as print on it any of the pictures you have uploaded onto your profile. If you use this feature, consider printing cards for each occasion separately. For example, you can print on your card, "We've met at Hedo in January 2010," or "You should remember us from Joe's party!"

Meet-and-Greets
By Larry and Mia

The more, the merrier...

Meet-and-Greet is one of the most common Lifestyle events. The name says it all: you meet like-minded people and make contact with them. Most of the time, M&Gs are hosted by swingers just like you who decided to contribute some of their own time for the Lifestylers to connect with each other and meet personally.

The majority of M&Gs happen in public places, mostly bars. Sometimes, hosts of the event have an agreement with the administration to close the venue doors to allow in an M&G's clientele only. Sometimes, the bar owner agrees to donate a certain period of time to M&G visitors exclusively, but, let's say, from 10 p.m. the bar becomes open to the ordinary public again.

If the venue belongs solely to the M&G crowd, you usually pay an entrance fee in addition to your obligation to buy drinks at the regular price. Besides other host expenses, this fee usually covers a specially hired security personnel who makes sure you are safe behind closed doors.

At other times, administration allows in regular public. Sometimes, venue owners have no idea about an M&G being in progress.

If an M&G takes place while the venue is also accessible for regular customers, the hosts have to come up with some procedure that enables you, the Lifestylers, to recognize each other while you still do not look unlike anyone else. You should have this secret modus operandi in your arsenal well before you arrive.

M&G hosts use a variety of signs to distinguish fellow swingers from vanilla people who happen to be around, including wrist or finger bands (colored or not) or accessories you both or just one of you wear in a certain way. Some use a code question, such as "Are you from Cinnabar Corporation?" If you answer, "Yes," the asking person knows you are here for the same reason.

At M&Gs, remember to dress-to-impress, yet to keep it on the moderate side. Even if the venue of an M&G did not allow the regular public in, you would not be able to dress overly provocatively since you are still at a *public* place. Attending an event at a public place requires you to behave by appropriate public standards and keep yourselves within the standards of vanilla decency. In addition, don't forget about all-vanilla venue staff, too.

At the M&G you will experience a shortage of sexual liberty. The good news is that you can compensate (at least partially) for this deficiency by the prospect of meeting many new people at the same time and place. Therefore, your chances of finding *the ones* for the night (and maybe more than ones, if you are lucky) are greatly higher than during couple-to-couple dates.

M&G's success depends on the hosts. It is problematic to expect a positive outcome from any get-together unless the hosts screened prospective attendees before sending invitations. All proposed guests should have something in common. Whoever performs an initial screening should at least use parameters such as involvement and age level (curiosity, soft swap, full swap, etc.). Like likes like!

Usually, you can figure out what to expect from the M&G in question based on the invitation itself. The hosts should let you know in advance what kind of people they target. If they won't, we advise skipping this event—it may waste your time. As an example, never hold the hosts responsible for your ruined expectations of meeting only couples at the M&G that permits single guys. Blame yourselves

Swinging from A to Z

instead for not paying adequate attention to the invitation and not performing minimal due diligence.

You should be pleased if you were lucky to meet an exciting couple at the M&G and managed to click with them. However, you should be prepared to take the action itself to the privacy of the nearest hotel or someone's home.

Swing clubs

By Larry and Mia

Nothing is impossible here!

Swing clubs represent an important branch of the swinging Lifestyle. Expect a broad variety of activities and wide range of attendees by any factor—age, race, nationality, swinging preferences, and so on.

Are swing clubs legal? In most European countries, they are. In the U.S., it depends on the state. In some states, they are legitimate businesses. In others, they have to keep a lower profile and position themselves as a kind of private club functioning on a members-only basis. This way the owners avoid public status and can drop the limitations related to proper behavior in public places for their patrons.

Several clubs have a liquor license so you would be able to buy alcohol right on the spot. As for soft drinks and mixers, they are usually included in the admission fee. Clubs that do not have a liquor license will allow you to BYOB. You could check your booze into the bar and club's bartender would serve you from your stash. Don't forget to tip.

Most of the clubs provide decent food. It varies from club to club and can be anything from light snacks to the full dinner course. Some exclusive clubs even have an à la carte menu and waiters.

One of any club's main attractions is the dance floor, whether it's small or huge. A DJ always plays the popular hits, and the sound is in the range from loud to very loud.

Several clubs allow single men on a permanent basis or on particular days only. Others do not allow them at all. Conversely, you can be sure that single ladies are always welcome, even if the given club positions itself as couples-only. Besides, many clubs accommodate single women (both escorted and not escorted by couples) free of charge.

The admission fee differs from venue to venue. Don't expect it to be cheap. We have found the average club visit costs $80 to $130 per couple. In addition, several clubs charge a membership fee. It could be a one-time charge on your first visit only or a time-dependent charge, once a quarter or once a year.

Off-premise clubs

By Larry and Mia

This is where the right mood suggests some further steps.

Off-premise clubs, as well as off-premise parties, do not provide actual playgrounds. In rare cases, some have more or less private areas for limited sexual activity. Never expect to see fully equipped playrooms with beds, etc. If you click with someone at an off-premise party, you take your actual play somewhere else.

Think of an off-premise party as of kind of M&G since at the core it still suggests its attendees getting acquainted and hooking up with each other. Yet, compared to an M&G, visiting an off-premise venue provides significant benefits. At an off-premise club you can drop the restrictions that apply to an M&G regarding both your appearance and behavior. You are no longer in public. You are now in a swinging-friendly environment where you don't have to keep your intentions a secret. In this case, club's employees (most might be vanilla) know what to expect and earn their salaries to support the clientele.

Since these kinds of events are for swingers or, at least, Lifestyle-friendly people with no vanilla public allowed, women may dress seductively. In fact, you are encouraged to do so. If you don't, you might feel uncomfortable. High heels, revealing outfits (from casual-sexy to dressy-sluttish), exotic wigs—anything you like and everything that makes you feel desirable would fit perfectly.

Expect a lot of dirty dancing and teasing: girl-to-girl, couple-to-couple, and group ones, lots of sex-related jokes, laughs, and mingling. Kissing strangers, some blowjobs and licking activities in darker corners are parts of the environment, too. Yes, these activities happen at off-premise events, but that is *all that happens*.

Some people visit off-premise clubs just to experience their onsite features. They are happy with what happens there and don't look for more. Others come expecting to make new connections, hence, planning to continue their fun right after the party.

Attending an off-premise event may cost more in total than an on-premise club visit since you may have to pay for the hotel room. Moreover, the costs of on-premise and off-premise club admissions don't differ significantly.

Keep in mind that off-premise clubs and events attract many curious and less-experienced people who feel safe enough at this atmosphere where no actual sex occurs. If you are beginners, an off-premise club is a good place to make your first Lifestyle statement. If you are seasoned swingers, you likely will have no interest in visiting.

Below is a part of a discussion that took place some time ago in the Internet group we manage for our friends. It reflects our group members' points of view on the subject of off-premise clubs and events.

MICS:
Is anyone going to a nude pool party this February third?
The theme for the party is Mardi Gras. The party hosts will e-mail additional info to all signed members.
ADMINISTRATORS [This is Larry & Mia]:
We looked up the info for this event and didn't get much detail. Is this a nude M&G, off-premise event, or on-premise one? It seems, at least two more CPLs from our group signed for this event. Folks, do any of you have an answer to the

above question? We would gladly attend, but this must be an on-premise thing. Nothing else works for us.

MICS:

Since this party is going to be in a health club, most likely it's going to be off-premise. You can contact the hosts and ask for more info. But then again, a wondering mind can always find a place to have fun after the party (or during), right?

ADMINISTRATORS:

We would prefer having sex in a bed, not on some kind of toilet.

RIGHTSIZE:

We aren't off-premise parties fans. What's the sense of getting all worked up with no place to play? Yes, I hear some of you say you can always go to a hotel or someone's house after. Yet, with family and vanilla world commitments, our Lifestyle time is precious, and we don't like to waste it on having sex in some unequipped place or drive around looking for a bed. It was fun when we were teenagers, but not now.

ADMINISTRATORS:

We could not say it better. Thanks for putting this together in a perfect way.

MICS:

Well, let me put it the way we see it: sex or no sex, it's still fun. Consider it as a nude pool party with some possible benefits. We are not into sex on the toilet or in some back room (nevertheless it sounds kinky, though) LOL! In no way we are promoting this party. We are not even sure whether we will go to it or we won't! This is just our opinion, and we hope we will have some pure naked fun (if we go).

VIXEN32:

Okay, here are our two cents. We do not attend off-premise parties because for us they are a waste of time and money. Still, we are glad they exist as they keep busy some of not serious crowd. There are plenty of on-premise parties and clubs in town.

Swinging from A to Z

They come and go. We absolutely prefer private parties. Second best for us are on-premise clubs.

RIGHTSIZE:

We totally agree with Vixen. Off-premise parties are a waste of time. We have been to one and only because it was free. Stayed for one hour and wound up leaving and going to our favorite on-premise club. Even though someone might consider us as "not serious," since we don't full swap, we do like to play after the dancing part.

On-premise clubs
By Larry

This is where the right mood is totally sufficient.

Let us call on-premise clubs just *clubs* from now on. It would adequately reflect our own position, since we only visit these kinds of clubs.

Visiting a club, especially for the first time, suggests your knowledge of what to expect there. And the truth is you can expect virtually anything.

First, you should be ready to observe provocative behavior, wild and wicked dancing, and revealing outfits. No other place in the world exists where it is more appropriate to look tempting than at a swing club. But you could see all these actions at off-premise clubs, too.

The difference? At on-premise event, you will witness *real* sexual encounters and a lot of partial and complete nudity (including the dance and bar areas). Just imagine you are watching porn, but watching it in reality, not on your TV screen. Besides, nobody restricts you from being a part of the scene. You can be the [porn] stars of this live movie yourselves. You can also be producers and directors of the show.

Clubs vary, but most have common features: a reception area (where you pay for your visit), coat check-in, bar and food areas, boisterous dance floor, security guards, and an inside smoking area. Expect separate gentlemen's and ladies' restrooms. Yet, as a rule, persons of any gender may use them both with no hesitation. Most locations offer showers as well as lockers (some venues require you to bring your own lock, though).

All clubs have a specially equipped play area(s) with several separate rooms or, alternatively, one large playroom. Most clubs provide beds, sofas, chairs, and other furniture, while at some you'll see just mats on the floor. In any case, sheets and towels will be clean. Many clubs supply robes and even disposable slippers. Some offer condoms, some don't, so always have them with you.

At some clubs, rules allow attendees to close playroom doors and, if you are outside, please don't open them! At other clubs, you won't find playroom doors at all.

Best swing venues prohibit their clients from attending play areas while being dressed. You must be naked or wearing nothing but a robe or towel to pass the security guard. This rule keeps away the annoying curious people who aren't able to take off their clothes. They sit at the bar fully dressed while swingers are having fun in the back. At such venues, if you are naked, you can be anywhere in the club, but access is limited if you are wearing clothes.

Usually, clubs open at 9 p.m. and stay open until 5 a.m. It is not a brilliant idea to arrive well before midnight since you would not want to find yourselves being one of the first visitors. On the other hand, if you have a first date scheduled at the club on that night, it's not a bad plan to meet there a little earlier, say at 11 p.m. A half-empty place without excessively loud music will give you a chance to talk with no rush and too much distraction. Most of the crowd arrives at about midnight, though. At 1 a.m., the club is blistering and blazing at full-force, and people start moving to playrooms.

Club strategies

By Larry and Mia

Sex is nature's way of saying "Hi!"
You are the best persons to take care of yourselves.

Let's be clear—you come to a swing club with certain expectations. Furthermore, everyone else is there with similar hopes. Nobody keeps his or her desires a secret from anyone, making the possibility of achieving your night's goal fairly high. You need only connect with the right people on the right level.

Your chances skyrocket if you choose to be active. Be as energetic as possible; don't wait for an opportunity to arrive. Create the opportunity yourselves.

Keep in mind, however, that your behavior still should not go beyond certain limits. Before moving any further on the subject, let's recall that golden Lifestyle rule—"No means No." Use it as needed, but don't be surprised if someone else uses it toward you. Even if you are sure you are a perfect-in-every-way couple, some people around will believe you are not. If they don't like you, never try to convince them, never insist, and never be persistent and pushy. Don't waste your and others' time, and don't create a situation where you asked to leave for inappropriate manners.

Several types of actions could provide you with the desired outcome. Some we personally find efficient. Since they represent our experience, we are taking the liberty of naming them our own way.

Dancing approach

This approach is the most natural and the most effective at the same time. You come close to people you are interested in on the dance floor. The ladies, if they like each other, will easily find their common moves. Body language is the best communication in the Lifestyle since swinging is all about the body. This language does not require any special translation, conversion, or re-definition. If desire is mutual, the dance instantly becomes a teasing contest where the guys will participate too. If it happens, just take it from there. If not, move on to the next couple you like.

Mingling-at-the-bar approach

Nothing here would be different from what you do at vanilla bars. Talk to people you like and try to match with them. The conversation should be rather sex-related and stimulating enough. Discuss your swinging preferences, share your Lifestyle experiences, etc. Just don't brag. Remember, your counterparts are here for the same reason you are. If they like you, they will express it one way or another. If you attract them sexually, they won't refuse to play with you. On the contrary, if they are not fascinated with the idea, move on.

You could (and should) apply the above two approaches in the initial club party phase. We would call this part *dressed-up* or *mingling*. If the party already has moved into its second phase, *naked*, and you did not yet come across your playmates-to-be, use other approaches while you are at the play area. They can work as a continuation of one (or both) of the above as well as by themselves. It is never too late while you are still at the club. We recall our own visit when we started to play with the couple at 4 a.m., and that was our first encounter for the night!

Fishing approach

This method is for more selective as well as more experienced swingers. Try to *catch your fish* while you are moving from one playroom to another or staying in the hallway. At this party stage, it is not hard to get an objective impression on any given couple since everyone is more or less naked. After you spot a couple you like, your better half should approach them and suggest having some fun together. She can make an offer either by literally asking or by using a body language. Make a pass on them by *accidental* (yeah, right!) or *on purpose* touching. A friendly hug will do as well. If they react positively, you are *there*, and your next step will be to find the closest available spot to play. If you are still shooting for more after that play has happened, you are free to approach another couple the same way.

This approach enables you to find partners in case you only like to play with particular people. As mentioned, you need to be skilled and enough experienced on the club scene to execute it. Still, it does not guarantee you will be busy this night.

Our friends Dirk and Lisa (the PR person mentioned earlier) visit clubs almost every week and mostly use this fishing approach. We would call Dirk and Lisa *professional* swingers. They started swinging while they were in their early 20s and still are in the Lifestyle now, more than 17 years later. They are selective and always prefer playing with most attractive people. Yet, even with their extreme club experience, sometimes they can't find play partners. We, too, had several empty nights while we were fishing.

If you are not overly selective or for some reason prefer to go for quantity rather than quality, the next method will be good for you. We employ this routine when we feel somewhat lazy. Besides, we are true fans of variety in the Lifestyle and try to get a little of everything. The outcome is always as expected—we never suffer from lack of attention using the following.

Relax-and-play approach

For it to work, you should move to the play area a bit earlier, while it is still not overcrowded. Lie down in the middle of the widest bed you can find and start playing with each other. Others will soon follow, and at some point, you will find yourselves in the middle of the action. All you need to do is to make a simple physical contact with the couple you like, which is easy while all of you are naked and are within a few-inch distance. Any gentle touch will work, but again, your lady should initiate.

Although you can attract more people with this approach, you do not risk anything, since the "No means No" rule still applies. If somebody you don't like touches you, you are free to reject him or her. Your play partners might not be as good as your model of perfection. Still, you two are in full control.

This approach, though, requires certain swinging experience, too. You must be completely uninhibited to use it, and it takes time in swinging to arrive to that state of mind. We find it a great fun since we never know whom we will play with next. Thanks to this approach, we got rid of the false impression that people's looks and sexual qualities have anything in common.

Swinging and jealousy
By Larry

Weird things just happen sometimes.

Unlike private parties, where the hosts do not invite everyone willing to attend, clubs accommodate nearly everyone. You can always expect different people: real swingers, swinging wannabes, curious watchers, experienced, and making their first steps. Thus, you have to be ready for everything. In particular, prepare to meet that green-eyed monster—jealousy.

Jealousy and swinging are incompatible to the core. Your relationship has no room for jealousy if you are in the Lifestyle. We've already talked about mutual trust, sharing, and accurate choices in swinging. All of that, used in the right way, should eliminate jealousy from the beginning.

So, why is this section here? Because besides your own relationship issues you might have already managed to sort out, you should be equipped to handle those of others and to react properly.

The folowing story is from the authors' past. The *naked* part of the club party was cooking. We had already played with a couple or two, yet were ready for more when an Israeli couple approached us. We did not ask their names, which happens at clubs all the time.

Strangely for us, the man was doing all the talking. His wife or maybe girlfriend (not sure) was just there, smiling. The man had a great tool, and Mia generally appreciates this quality in men. After a minute, we came to that mutual agreement and moved to the playroom. The man and Mia went straight to bed and started having fun. I tried to do so with the lady, but she declined my attempts. I was not too frustrated. I was aware of couples where their better halves just accompany their partners to clubs and parties for them to play while watching themselves. It was fine with me. As long as my wife had fun (and it looked like she was having a great time), I could just sit and watch her with my great pleasure.

Mia was moaning on the bed with the man on top of her, having fun. I sat on the sofa and the lady was staying at the door, both of us watching. After 10 minutes, the woman came close to the bed and said something to her man in Hebrew. He answered her. She said something in return and left the room. She came back with their friends, another Israeli couple. This time a little longer conversation ensued between all four of them. They were talking in Hebrew, which I didn't understand. At the time, the man continued playing with Mia as if nothing was happening. As for Mia, she was half-unconscious, which often happens when she is playing.

The company, including the lady herself, left. In about seven or eight minutes (the mutual fun was still in progress), she came in fully dressed, with her coat on, proceeded to the bed, and smacked her man in the head with her hand. The punch was powerful and the man finally stopped. I was on my feet near the bed, and Mia came back to reality, too.

While the woman was proudly carrying herself out of the room, Mia said to the man, "It looks like she is mad at you. You are having a huge problem!" He replied, "Don't worry, there are no problems anymore. She left! Let's continue. I'd like to do it for at least two more hours!" We said goodnight right at that moment.

So, what has happened? Apparently, the woman was prepared to approve her partner's individual fun initially. She just could not stand the situation after watching him for some time with a *beautiful* woman who *enjoyed* the ride. "Beautiful" and "enjoyed" are the keywords here. From our swinging experience, some ladies are perfectly fine for their husbands to play with average-looking and average-performing women. However, they become jealous if their halves play with "better-quality" partners. We've had several situations on our way where ladies of the couple refused us just because Mia is too stunning and over-enticing sexually.

The next incident when a lady smacked her man in the face over Mia paradoxically happened at the same club on our very next visit and in the same playroom. This time, it took place even before we all clicked, as soon as the well-hung gentleman hugged Mia and tried to kiss her. And we saw this couple play with others right before it had happened!

Our friends Dirk and Lisa, who witnessed both episodes, joked afterward, "Guys, from now on it will be easy to identify all the hung males at the club. All we have to do is to make a note on everyone who is punched in the face the moment you two are entering the door!"

We never play with just half a couple anymore if the other half does not participate. Yes, while at the club, we still prefer to find a couple with a well-hung male, but that is not our main point anymore. Plenty of exclusive single gentlemen are in the Lifestyle, and singles are easier to deal with. No one is around to fight over them, which made us start dating "special" single males in addition to couples.

If the man of the couple does all the preliminary talking alone, something is likely wrong with this couple. You can easily end up in an unpleasant situation.

If it doesn't want to get up
By Larry

This is between us men.

Although erectile problems pertain exclusively to gentlemen, I welcome the ladies to read this section as well. Women should consider this information far from excessive. What's more, they have a right to know.

Gentlemen, please be aware: even if you never had any difficulties with your life partner or while playing couple-to-couple, it could knock on your door while in group situations. I've seen it happen and I have experienced it personally.

We hadn't had a group setting background, just many couple-to-couple ones, at the time of our first swing club visit. It was completely unexpected and frustrating to me when I discovered I was simply unable to perform in the club scene. During our first few club visits, I tried all the erectile dysfunction (ED) medications one-by-one, but none helped.

My problem seemed to be mental. At that moment when I encountered myself in the middle of a naked crowd, I turned impotent. We even considered ending our swing club visits. Yet, every time I insisted on trying it one more time. My determination helped.

My first successful performance happened on our fifth club visit. Maybe I was able to relax enough and finally stopped paying attention to watching people around, maybe I got used to the environment; I am not sure. Nonetheless, I never had impotence since.

Men's failure can happen to anyone, at any time, and at any circumstances. It is nothing to be ashamed of. It takes place in reality more often than you can imagine. It is rather commonplace in the swinging Lifestyle. ED can occur because of performance anxiety, inexperience, overexcitement, or just too much alcohol.

Once we hosted a gangbang with four couples and 10 gentlemen. All guys we invited were in their 20s and 30s. Five guys were new to us. Three did not have any group experience, and two out of those three could not perform.

Ladies, please realize that a particular man's temporary inability to perform has nothing to do with you personally. It's not about how you look or how desirable you are. Remember, the main difference between women and men is that women are always capable of having sex, but far from always want to, while men always want to, but, unfortunately, are not always capable.

Ladies may be able to help rather than just move on. Simple stroking and giving head may be a solution. If our ladies are willing and are motivated enough, they can do miracles.

During one of our club visits, a couple approached us and offered to play. At that time, I was not optimistic about my ability to perform since we already had a lot of play, and I was *done* twice. I told so to the lady of the couple. She replied, "Don't worry, honey, I'm not 16, I know what to do!" It took her about 15 or 20 minutes to get me back *in shape*. However, she managed to accomplish the *task* to our common pleasure!

What should a man do if his tool is tired? Continue trying, but relax, smile, and keep in mind, there is always a next time. This prescription worked just fine for everyone we know who had similar difficulty in the past. It should go away eventually.

However, do not expect any woman to stimulate you all night long. You must be respectful. Excuse yourself, let her go to have fun with others, and never make a big deal out of it. Nobody will ever refuse you in the future because you could not get it up in the past.

Private parties
By Larry and Mia

Not everyone is welcome here.

The basic activities at the private swing party don't significantly differ from the swing club. The difference is in the managing of club events vs. private parties. Since someone hosts a party privately, this person establishes, enforces, and supports all the rules and regulations for the event.

Parties can vary widely by attendees' qualities, age, swinging interests, and preferences. The hosts make their party what they want it to be. Nevertheless, all private parties have something in common: they cater to a select group of people rather than everyone. No matter what the hosts have in mind, they always have to carry out an initial screening of their prospective attendees before sending invitations. Depending on the type of party and planned activities, this screening can be more or less tough.

Parties without pre-screening cannot be successful by default. Swingers value their fun time and prefer to save it for events in which they know what to expect.

So, how does this screening physically work? If you intend to visit a private party, be prepared to answer some questions. Don't worry; there is nothing personal. Nobody asks for your private information besides your names (and you are free to provide fake ones if you prefer).

These questions are usually like:

"How old are you?"

"How long have you been in the Lifestyle?"

"What are your sexual fantasies?"

"What are your swinging preferences?"

"What kind of swinging experience do you have?"

Answer honestly. Never lie (maybe just a little!) to people about your age. Nobody will ever invite you a second time if you do. Also, never give others the wrong information about your experience. Your deceit will backfire on you.

Most hosts will want to see your photograph(s). It should not be anything kinky, in most cases "G-rated" face and body pictures will work. Some hosts will prefer to see both of you together on the same photo to make sure you are in fact a couple.

Realize that screening is a two-way street. Along with the screening the hosts perform on you, you should try to match the proposed party to your own ideas. Do not hesitate to ask hosts any questions you would like to. If they do not respond, better forget about their event.

Someone can host a swing party at a hotel (hotel party) or at their house (house party). Those kinds are identical except for location. For the house party, you are joining the hosts at their private home. At hotel parties, depending on the expected number of attendees, the hosts would invite you into a one-bedroom, two-bedroom, or three-bedroom suite or into the connected-to-one-another array of single rooms. Sometimes they even book a whole hotel floor.

Parties can be *commercial* or *profit-free (non-commercial)*. But don't confuse them with *paid* and *free* parties. A non-commercial party is not necessarily free. It can have an admission charge. Still, the hosts would calculate this charge to cover their related to the party expenses, no more and no less.

Commercial and non-commercial swing parties significantly differ. However, the disparity is not about the money you pay. It's rather about what you tend to expect from these two kinds of parties in terms of possible situations you encounter while attending.

Commercial swing parties
By Larry and Mia

This is where the hosts almost never play themselves.

Yes, the hosts do not have time to play at commercial swing parties. They are counting the money. Besides, often they are not swingers at all.

Some of these parties can be good, some not that good. You can evaluate any Lifestyle event by several parameters, such as premises, food, music, and drinks selection. However, those parameters are all secondary compared to *the crowd* the given event attracts. The hosts manage a guest list by inviting people based on some criteria they have in mind for their events. Therefore, everything depends on the hosts.

True, if you are in a position of hosting a swing party for profit, you will be interested in sending as many invitations as possible. From this standpoint alone, you would not care much for the screening process. From the other side, you should keep in mind your guests' overall satisfaction. If people are not happy with your events, they won't come back. Furthermore, they'll share their thoughts with friends, and friends with their friends. Eventually, word of mouth will destroy your business. The Lifestyle crowd talks.

Therefore, as a host, you will need to find a correct formula that could support your guests' fun and, at the same time, will generate enough profit.

We have visited commercial parties (mostly at hotels) several times. Once we bumped into the chaos of an unscreened crowd. There were watchers, full-swappers, soft-swappers, couples of dramatically different ages, and the curious. In addition, the hosts overcrowded the place having about 20 couples in two adjoining hotel rooms with two queen beds in each. We did not even try to start playing under these circumstances; we just left. Those hosts tried to promote their parties and throw them regularly, but after three or four months we noticed their ads disappeared.

We had a few not bad experiences at commercial parties as well. Each time it happened where the crowd was homogeneous, at least by age and physical attractiveness. As for us, we prefer visiting swing clubs rather than commercial parties. At least we know what to expect in return for our money.

The premises at swing clubs are more suitable for swinging activities. Other than that, commercial parties are not any different from clubs. The reason for this similarity is, again, a superficial level of screening.

Non-commercial parties
By Larry and Mia

This is where you get pleasure for the sake of pleasure.

If someone ever invites you to a profit-free private party, the authors implore you to accept the invitation. If the hosts do not charge for attendance, they *only* invite people they like. It almost guarantees guests will fit the group profile.

We hosted our house parties for years and never for profit. We started long ago with get-togethers for four or five couples. Our parties have grown and have become themed events with nearly 40 people attending (maximum capacity of our house). These events are hard to get into. We handpick our circle of friends who always serve as the base for our guest list.

Each time we do invite new people since swinging is all about fresh faces (and bodies). Nevertheless, these new people are either our own discovery or referrals from friends. Not every new couple fits into our group's common fun scenario, and we don't ask them back in this case. We just save these people from being frustrated while protecting our friends from possible dissatisfaction. As the hosts, we strive for quality and our group's good time.

Our overall objectives are:
- Everyone at our parties is within a certain age group.
- Everyone is intelligent, attractive, reliable, and polite.
- Everyone shares the same swinging philosophy. All are no-drama hard-core swingers.

If you received an invitation to a non-commercial party, judge what to expect by the party hosts themselves. Remember, they host for their own pleasure. You can be sure all the guests will fall within the hosts' Lifestyle preferences. The well-known proverb, "Tell me who your friend is and I'll tell you who you are" we would rephrase to "Tell me who the hosts are, and I'll tell you what kind of [swinging] friends they have."

A few years ago, we attended a huge party hosted by our Hedo friend at his summerhouse located in a high-status area. The theme for the event was a Medieval Ball. The hosts, our friend and his girlfriend, encouraged every guest (they invited about 60 couples) to dress appropriately and informed that they would not allow anyone into the house otherwise.

When we arrived at the property gate, a security guard dressed as a medieval warrior stood under the huge banner with a knight's emblem on it. He checked our invitation and allowed us to proceed.

The second security (in a similar outfit) parked our car, collected our invitation, and informed the in-house staff of our arrival using a mobile radio device. On entering the house, a PA announced, "Sir Larry and Lady Mia have entered the chambers!" Two paid actors dressed as jokers played trumpets and the hosts formally greeted us. Every guest was dressed according to the theme. As well as every member of the specially hired service staff was, including the bartender (there was an open bar). The food was exceptional, from the roasted pig to exotic desserts.

After a couple of hours of eating, drinking, and mingling, guests proceeded to the huge backyard transformed into a medieval knights' contest field. Knights (other actors) were riding horses, shooting arrows, competing with swords, etc. The show went on for more than an hour.

At about 11 p.m. the hosts invited everyone to a specially equipped playhouse in the back of the property where all the adult activities took place. The play part of the event was exciting, too, but not that memorable compared to all the above.

Every profit-free party is unique; every host has different requirements and preferences. Some concentrate on food (we don't), some on entertainment or dancing (we don't), and some mostly on playtime itself (we do).

If you are ever up to hosting your own parties
By Larry

Let's assume you wish to host at your house. Where do you start?

First, figure out how many guests you will be able to accommodate comfortably. The number depends on several factors such as the amount of money you wish to invest and your playroom features, including its maximum capacity.

Depending on what you would like to achieve, your expenses could vary, yet the following ones are typical for any party:

- Cost of food, soft drinks, and mixers. That is, if your party is BYOB. If not, add the cost of wine, beer, and hard liquor.
- Cost of disposable items (condoms, candles, caps, plates, forks, spoons, tissues, napkins, trash bags, etc.).
- Cost of pre-party and after-party house cleanup, including laundry expenses.

In our experience, for a BYOB party of 30 to 40 people you would need to spend $400 to $500.

For the play area, you can use any room (or several rooms) of your house. You only need an appropriate quantity of mattresses or mats (air beds will do, too), some seating furniture, and dimmable lighting fixtures. One queen-size mat is enough for three to four couples; not everyone is playing at the same time.

Second, you need to invite people. The best approach here is "quality rather than quantity." You only want people who contribute to your party's goal, so screen, screen, and screen. Make sure all your guests are of the same swinging preferences, same age group, and same intellectual level. They should like each other or else it won't work!

Third, establish your party rules and regulations. Make sure they all are included in the final invitation you send to every guest. Instead of giving guidelines one-by-one, below is the text of our recent party invitation. If you like it, feel free to use any part of it.

> Dear friends,
>
> Please confirm the receipt of this invitation and do not hesitate to ask any questions you may have. Believe us, we've done a lot of admin work to bring together all of you at our house and would like to be sure all of our guests safely received this e-mail and are ready to go.
>
> So, please hit the "reply" button with just one word "yes" and sign your names.
>
> **Example:**
> Yes! John and Mary.

If you wish to add something like, "Larry & Mia, we love you and miss you guys," we would accept that as well!

Important:

If there are last-minute changes of your plans and you are unable to come, please let us know using the phone number below. We won't be online starting at least two days before the party. We would like to avoid waiting for people who won't come!

Party theme:

It is "Pajama & Lingerie Night."

Please, as usual, support our theme and dress code accordingly. Don't be any different; you might feel uncomfortable! If you were unable to find a proper PJ or Lingerie outfit (yeah, right!) at least dress to impress! The Lifestyle is a show, so play your role decently. Besides, this night might provide you with your best memories and most interesting stories you will tell your pals at the nursing home!

Party time:

Mouths open - 8:00 p.m.

Legs close - ?

We kindly ask you to be on time and do not miss the fun. For new people: it is important to know our parties are quite different compared to the ones you attended so far. If we invite people at eight, we expect them to come at eight! Forget about being an hour or two later as a sign of a proper attitude. It does not work for our group and us personally. We have hosted parties for years, and all our regulars are reliable, which is one of our selection criteria. At the same time, we all are completely uninhibited and do not require much time to get naked (another selection criteria).

Therefore, please be sure that after two hours, we just have to invite our guests to the playroom, or else they start playing right at the reception area. (We still would like to situate all the sexual activities at the playroom only!) Besides, you definitely don't want to come to a house full of naked people and start playing right away without proper introductions and a little mingling and giggling with your partners-to-be.

Please allow yourself more driving time. If, by any chance, you arrive earlier, just come inside. We'll be up from 6 a.m., we promise!

Party schedule:

8:00 - 9:00 Meet old friends and make new ones.

9:00 - 9:20 Dance floor. (Based on previous experience, this part never lasted more than 20 minutes, sorry!).

9:20 - 9:45 Guests and hosts show. Blow job contest. We reserved a prize for our Sucking Queen.

9:45 - ? Playroom is open. Hosts are not responsible for the party anymore since they are now regular attendees.

Objective warning:

We won't be able to answer the entry door once the party moves to the playroom. Your hosts prefer to participate in the action rather than sit at the door with the phone in hand and wait for still missing guests' royal entrance!

We hope we explained fully the time-related issue and it is now clear.

Donations:

Let us disappoint some of you (yeah, right again!), but we accept no donations. Our parties are completely free of charge events. As such, we can invite only guests who are of our kind. Thanks to this policy, our parties are (we've heard from other people) one of the best in terms of crowd, one of the hardest to get in, and one of the greatest judging by our friends' sexual experiences.

Attendance:

We are having 17 couples, six gentlemen, and three ladies confirmed. They are in the age range from their 20s to their 40s. Our guests are coming from New York, New Jersey, Pennsylvania, Massachusetts, and Florida (sorry, no one from California this time).

As all our friends know, we never expose attendees-to-be, even to each other. It would not be acceptable for us morally. What's more, a little surprise never hurts. Believe us, it is our great pleasure to see old friends meeting after some time apart from each other. Besides, it is even more pleasurable to see how excited all of you are if you can see new attractive faces around. If you like some other guests, don't forget to ask them for their contact information. We do not release such information and never will.

To our first-time guests (yes, we invited some, as usual):

Please make yourselves at home. All our friends and the hosts strive to make you feel at ease. In fact, our first-timers are luckier than regulars are. They have more attention and respect. Sorry, old buddies, but you have to agree and accept this.

Food, drinks, and other collateral items:

Light finger food and soft drinks are available on a serve yourself basis.

BYOB (bottle), BYOC (condoms), BYOT (towels).

For those who are not sure: "BYO" usually stands for "bring your own." (LOL!)

Rules:

Based on our hosting experiences, we would like to stress the following three rules we established for your own safety:

Absolutely no drinks or food in the playroom!

Dispose used condoms and any unneeded articles into trash containers provided!

No cameras and phones in the playroom!

Other things to consider:

While you are on the outside deck, keep your clothes on and your voices much lower for our party to appear to our neighbors just like a vanilla one. While we really don't care what neighbors think, we still have concerns of a possible call to the police for disturbance.

We are sure police officers would find several friendly ladies to melt them down, yet we still would like to keep it as private as possible. Thanks in advance for all your consideration and cooperation. BTW, we are having some police officers among our guests, but please don't say a word to anyone!

Address/directions:
[The authors have left this part blank intentionally]

Parking:
Make sure to park on the left (our) side of the street only. The street is too narrow to park on both sides. Neighbors might not be able to pass and, instead, might try to join our party. Yet, they are pretty ugly; you don't want to play with them!

Do not park in the driveway unless you have a confirmation for overnight stay. It is not easy to ask naked people to move their cars at 3 a.m. to let you out!

If you get lost:
XXX.XXX.XXXX - Larry's cell
See you on Sat, the third of April, 8 p.m. sharp!
Kisses to all,
Larry & Mia

Finally, you must figure out how to *start* a party! In this context, starting a party means starting the party's main, i.e. *naked,* part.

One of our friends said, "The hardest part of any [swing] party is moving from the table to the bed." We could not agree more. If you allow your event to develop on its own, it could move in the wrong direction. After some time dedicated to talking and dancing, the party should logically progress into the playroom. You, as the hosts, should be able to pick the right moment for this event transformation and make the conversion itself natural and as easy for everyone as possible.

To take full control of the situation, we perform some entertainment or contests to involve the guests in the action and provide both participating and watching people an opportunity to ease up and emotionally prepare themselves.

The following are a few of our own latest developments in this area:

Runway show

We select three people for a jury panel. The participants walk the runway (carpet-covered pathway in our case) while presenting themselves in their outfits. The jury names the best gentleman and the best lady. We honor the winners with prizes, and they perform dirty dancing together.

Lesbian show

Group of ladies equipped with various toys, including dildos, double-headers, and strap-ons performs a short 10-minute show.

Blowjob contest

We sit five gentlemen in the middle of the room and blindfold them. Five ladies have exactly one minute for each gentleman and try to apply their best skills. The gentlemen cannot touch the ladies and have no idea which ladies are participating and in what order. All we tell them is the number of the current contestant. We name and award the "Sucking Queen" by summing up the guys' individual judgments on which number was the best.

Blowjob contest (variation)

All the rules and flow are the same as above, only this time the gentlemen know which ladies are involved into the contest. The gentlemen are the contestants now. We ask them to guess which girl we assigned to each number. We pronounce and prize the winner—the gentleman with the most correct matches. (If you think finding out who is who is easy, you are wrong. I once participated and didn't recognize my own wife because she intentionally changed her technique.)

Striptease with benefits

Mia performs a striptease dance with a twist: each time she takes off a piece of her outfit, all the guests have to take one off as well.

Best pleasing team contest

Three blindfolded guys lay down on the floor naked. Three teams consisting of two ladies each have two minutes for every gentleman. Again, guys cannot touch and don't know who is who. The gentlemen's summary vote defines a winning team.

As you can guess, after any of these performances all you need to do as the hosts is to invite your guests to the playroom.

Lastly, if you decide to have any contests, you have to prepare proper prizes for the winner(s). These prizes should be something with a Lifestyle meaning. In addition, don't forget to add the cost of prizes to your overall party expense calculation.

We wish you good luck!

Optimal M/F balance at parties

By Mia

> *The more orgasms a woman has, the more she will enjoy them...The more she "primes the pump," the more facile she becomes, and the more interested in sex she remains.*
> —Dr. Theresa Crenshaw

Here is another non-obvious item.

One more factor that is important for party success is a proper male/female balance.

Below is the part of our discussion with the hosts of a meet-and-greet within the private group on one of the websites:

Original Posting:

B152 [Website ID of the M&G host couple]
We are hosting a Saturday night Meet and Greet. Couples and single ladies are welcome. We also will allow couples to sponsor single males they know personally, but we limit the number of attending guys to a maximum of five. There will be music and soft mood lighting, lounge seating. We provide some finger food.

Private party: 6 p.m. – 9:30 p.m. Then the bar will be open to the regular public, yet we are all welcome to stay.

Contact our profile if interested.

FunTimes69 [This is the authors' site ID]
Just out of curiosity, why are there always-hard restrictions on single guys? We host parties for years and had a chance to learn that a perfect m/f balance has nothing to do with situations when there are more ladies than gentlemen. In reality (that is, of course, if the hosts are concerned of ladies' satisfaction), numbers should be quite opposite. We always have about 20% more gentlemen than ladies, and this ratio proves itself being just perfect for everyone.

We agree that keeping away guys from the street is a right move. Yet, if some couple or single lady is able to bring a respectful gentleman who is a great player as well (and with the right equipment), why limit single guys attendance to just five?

Why refrain from inviting single gentlemen approved by couples and, in fact, their Lifestyle friends for common use? We have more than a dozen perfect and outstanding-in-every-way guys whom we could recommend to everyone interested without the slightest doubt. For playing, most women need more attention and action than most men. Remember, we are talking about swinging ladies, not vanilla ones. So, why go against nature?

This posting illustrates the authors' position. An average swinging lady in most cases would need more than she could get from an average swinging gentleman, which makes single male swingers necessary for a party's success.

You won't gain much by adding another *ordinary* man, two, or three, though. Instead, there should be *exclusive* gentlemen, the kind hardly found as part of couples. Look for personality, intelligence, respect, reliability, great body, special "gear," and immense stamina.

What would happen to men of the couples if extra single guys were invited? Would our husbands and boyfriends have to cut down on their own participation? Would they have less fun? The answer to these questions is "No, they wouldn't!"

In fact, our own men would have even more fun. Because extraordinary single men are the reason we, women, get over-excited from the first party stage. This extra enthusiasm, in turn, provides our life partners with additional sexual opportunities and added thrills. Often enough, there is no need for the party warming-up stage in this case. As for the real fun, it starts earlier and lasts much longer.

You will be surprised to find out what we women are capable of when we are at the top of our sexual excitement.

Single males and single females in the Lifestyle

By Larry and Mia

Adding to the pleasure and sharing the fun.

The Lifestyle accommodates many single men and women. But many fewer ladies than gentlemen—about 20 times less.

Vast numbers of singles claim to be swingers but are not. Swing websites are overwhelmed with single profiles, mostly males. Some people believe establishing their own profile on such a website opens the door to the swinging world. They think offering themselves for sex is all it takes, and some get mad when rejected. They are pushy, disrespectful, even violent from the moment they first contact you. Most swingers are tired of the guys who rudely IM and send e-mails with complete disregard to what our profiles are referring to. Many profiles state "No single guys!" for this reason.

Besides the Web, single guys may cause trouble in the real world. Our friends and we had experiences with the bad guys who ruin it for all the good ones out there. We visited some parties and M&Gs where guys pushed and annoyed everyone, including those who had no interest in them. Sometimes, these guys come without invitation. Some of them walk the hallways of the nearest hotels in search of after-parties and try to work their way in.

There is also a group of single gentlemen and ladies who are not looking for couples at all. They use swing websites as kind of vanilla dating databases to find other singles. Yes, they are looking for sex, but not recreational, not open sex. Therefore, they are not swingers by definition.

Let's forget about these pseudo-swingers and talk about real respectful people interested in Lifestyle activities. More than enough singles are seeking couples and groups of couples to connect with sexually. This is how the swinging starts for them and this is where their Lifestyle entry point is.

If you are single and willing to become a player in the Lifestyle scene, realize that the success or failure depends on your willingness to stick with the common rules the Lifestyle has, and with the private rules of the couples you contact.

Singles in the Lifestyle play a *secondary* role. They are there to support couples, to add some spice to the fun. Hence, singles never command, control, or dominate a situation. This does not mean the Lifestyle discriminates against single swingers. Couples welcome them as equals at playtime. The big difference occurs in the way singles should approach and react to being approached, especially the single gentlemen.

The following is our e-mail exchange with a single gentleman who had contacted us not long ago. We are sorry for some explicit words that are impossible to take out of the context.

NiceStud:

Love your profile. I would like to point you to mine. Please let me know what you think. Hope to hear from you. Alan

FunTimes69:

Hi, Alan, and thanks for your interest. Please look at our requirements for single guys on our group profile "XXXSessions" on this website. If you are sure you are a match, we would like to see your "private area" pictures in addition to those you allowed us to view. Hope you don't mind; this is a swingers' site. L & M

NiceStud:

I read your requirements and believe I meet them all: under 40, 6'4", 225 (athletic), 8.5 thick circumcised inches. I will send pictures to your e-mail address. I never have had issues performing in front of a group; it is actually a turn-on for me. It has always been.

FunTimes69:

Thank you for your pictures. You are in the prospective TO-DO list. List is not short, so be patient. We never invite guys we don't know to our events right away; rather, they have to pass a "test drive" first—LOL. Some of our friends referring to us or we personally will contact you on the initial date within one or two months. It is often spontaneous and on a short notice. If you are flexible enough, it will definitely increase your chances for faster involvement with our group. Kisses, Larry & Mia

[The authors: Alan did not answer the last e-mail. Yet, since the guy was good looking, we decided to bypass his initial evaluation and invite him to our small party.]

FunTimes69:

Hi, Alan. We are having a little get-together (five to seven couples) at our friends' house next Saturday, at 8 p.m. Please let us know ASAP if you wish to join us. You only have three days to decide. Hugs, L & M

[The authors: Alan read this above e-mail the same day. We know this because the website marks every e-mail with date/time of its opening. Three days have passed with no reply from Alan.]

FunTimes69:

Alan, as you know, reliability is the key for our group members. It looks like this is not a part of your personality, though. Just to remind you, we expect answers to our e-mails in a timely manner. Let us know ASAP for us to plan accordingly. L & M

NiceStud:

L&M, your mail revealed a lot about you. I'm not into the whole "you're a single guy, i.e. you're worthless" bullshit. There are plenty of hot pussy/groups out there to fuck, as I am sure you know. And you may even be honest enough to admit it is probably harder to come by a good-looking, fit, hung, clean, D/D free, nice guy with stamina than a couple with a wife who wants to get fucked! So writing me a mail like the one you just did, shows you don't get it. Who do you think you are? What's next? Will you command me to answer? What a fucking joke! Go look for guys that are more desperate. Kind Regards, Alan

FunTimes69:

Alan, now it is clear why your profile does not have any certifications for all that significant time you are on this website. To remind you: we did not contact you. You contacted us. We've provided you with our requirements and you confirmed you accept them. BTW, reliability stays first in the list of our preferences! We invited you to our party, you did not answer for three days. Now, according to you, we are the bad guys! We suggest you to concentrate on your attitude. You have a lot of work to do in this area. We are always ready to meet nice and intelligent people. However, we are not up to accepting rudeness and egocentricity, no matter how great their possessor's outer shelf might be. You are so out!

Single swingers should have several qualities. Reliability and being gentle and polite are on the top of the list. As you can see, a mindset similar to Alan's is far from tolerable.

Frankly, singles (especially men) cannot afford to be overly selective because so many of them are available. Besides, not every Lifestyle couple accepts singles.

We have many single swinging friends of both sexes; all of them managed to join our group because they were respectful from the beginning, reliable, and friendly. They accepted the rules (including our internal group's rules) and followed them exactly the way our couples did.

Todd of Todd and Elena, a well-known Lifestyle couple who own the *LoveVoodoo* swing website, gave us a permission to quote his "Single men's guide to the Lifestyle" that we find interesting.

1. If you are 60 and you think you are going to pick up a 25-year-old hot lady on a Lifestyle site, unless you drive a Ferrari, have a big ass boat, and a house in South Beach, do not even bother reading on. Either keep your profile to look at pictures, or cancel it and move on. I cannot help you.
2. If you are overweight and out of shape, the chances of getting a hot lady are slim. Either lower your standards or go the gym and eat more salad. I am not trying to be mean; I have packed on a few extra pounds the last few years myself. But there are some great-looking guys out there that work out every day. Why would a lady want to have sex with you rather than them? You say you are a nice guy with a charming personality? Nice, but that is why they have husbands and boyfriends. You are not going to enter the Daytona 500 in a Caravan. If you do you will look like an ass.
3. I know you want to meet a nice single lady. Well, it is possible, I actually met Elena in the Lifestyle, but it is highly unlikely. If that is what you are looking for, I suggest you join a regular dating site, find the wildest lady you can, then get her into the Lifestyle!
4. Shave your balls! Stop laughing...Really...Shave your junk! First, it makes your dick look bigger. Second, it is just plain rude not to! Go ahead, do it now.

5. Dick pics. There is nothing I hate worse than getting up every morning to approve a hundred dick pics. Come on guys! It is just ridiculous. No one wants to see that. People just think you are a pervert when they see that. Are there exceptions? Yes. If you have a huge dick, I mean huge—over nine inches, then by all mean put up a couple of cock shots. I am sure you will get some action. If you are an average guy, keep it in your pants until it's time to use it!
6. Profile photos. Put some photos of you having a good time with friends—maybe taking part in some sort of sport, traveling, etc., or maybe a pic with a hot girl, not a porn star at AVN, just a regular hot girl. Other women will think, "Mmm... if he is good enough for her, he is good enough for me!" For God's sake, no pics of you sitting in front of your computer staring into the camera! Those are the worst.
7. Dress nice. Better to over-dress than under-dress. A nice pair of slacks, and a nice shirt, or a cool pair of jeans and a modern shirt will do fine. No Dockers and polo shirts, women will think you are boring and you have not been out in the last 20 years. No ratty jeans or T-shirts. If I have to explain why this is a bad idea, you are a lost cause. No tweed coats with patches on the sleeves! Seriously, go out spend a few hundred bucks. You have to look nice; there is a lot of competition out there.
8. No stupid screen names about how good you are orally. Please do not mention how big your tongue is in your profile. You might think, "Man, the ladies are going to love this! They love getting the oral, and they are going to be hot when they read this." No dude, they are not going to be hot; they are going to think, "Mmm, he talks about oral so much, I bet he has a small dick." You know why they will think that? Because they are probably right.
9. Never, ever get drunk. First, you act like an ass. Second, your thing will not work. Enough said.

10. Smoking in my opinion is a bad idea. I know, for Elena it is a deal breaker. Some people will not mind, however, but no one is going to say, "I would love to have sex with that guy, if he only smoked!" Play it safe, and don't smoke. On top of that it gives you bad breath and baked bean teeth, but this is only my opinion.
11. If you see a couple with a hot girl, always, approach the guy first and introduce yourself. Compliment his wife to him, and then introduce yourself to her. This is the toughest part. If you act like you are getting his permission, she may be offended. She may think, "Who does he think he is? If he wants to talk to me he should talk to me!" Then again, if you ignore him he may shut you down before you get started. I would hang back, observe the situation, and then tread lightly. The first contact is critical.
12. If things are going well, don't be shy. Ask her to dance, touch her, go for a kiss if you can get it. Elena calls this "respectfully aggressive." If you touch her in front of her guy, he will know that you are up front and not trying to do anything behind his back. I would then compliment him again, "You are a lucky guy," "Man, she can dance," etc.
13. Never ever approach a girl as soon as her guy walks away. This is a big NO. If it happens by accident, as soon as the guy comes back, be sure to shake his hand and introduce yourself.
14. If a girl approaches you, first thing I would ask is, "Who are you hear with?" If she is there with someone, ask her to introduce you. You can make big points doing this! If she is alone, you have just found the mythical unicorn; it is your lucky night!
15. Never tell anyone who you partied with. There is a stigma attached to partying with single men. If you are good, girls will tell each other. The word will get around. They will also know you can keep your mouth shut. This is key!

Swinging from A to Z

16. Participate in blogs and chats on swing sites. Talk about something interesting, but not controversial. No religion or politics.
17. If you go to a club, don't just stand there like a fool. If you do nothing, nothing will happen. Dance, talk to people, have fun!
18. Don't talk about how much money you make. It would not hurt to let people know you are successful, but don't be cocky about it. Maybe the couple is poor and the husband has a job making $35K a year. Then you come rolling in talking about how you just blew $35K playing craps in Vegas. You may make the husband feel bad, so he will not want to party.
19. Don't talk to the husband too much. Anyone who knows me knows I like to talk! A couple of times, I have approached a couple hoping to hook up with the girl. I found out I have a lot in common with the husband, and we started talking about cars or politics. Before I knew it, the wife was out dancing with someone else!
20. No gold chains or too much jewelry.
21. Save the dirty talk for the bedroom. It is a turn-on to some women but a turnoff to others. Why take a chance?
23. If you observe a couple, and there seems to be some tension, stay away. Nothing good could come out of approaching them. However, if he gets pissed and leaves her at the club alone, well, that's another story!
24. No means no. If you get the green light, go for it. But if a couple seems disinterested, tell them it was a nice meeting and move on. It is hard to kick a reputation for being pushy.
25. Finally, if you cannot get laid in a vanilla bar, you cannot get laid in a swingers club. Most of the time, a vanilla club is an easier place for a single guy. Swingers clubs are about having a unique experience, not easy pussy. If that what you are looking for, you just don't get it, and no swing site is going to help you.

Chapter 7

Swing Resorts & Conventions

Hedo mania

By Larry and Mia

Be wicked for a week!

Hedonism resorts, Hedonism II and Hedonism III, sited on the beautiful island of Jamaica both belong to SuperClubs' chain. To answer a frequent question, Hedonism I never existed.

Hedonism II was the first one historically and celebrated its 25th anniversary not long ago. It is definitely the most notorious resort in the whole world. "Swingers' Paradise," "Lifestyle Bomb," "Place Where Everything is Possible," "Flagship of the Swinging World," "*All-Inclusive Resort*"—those are just a few of its dubs you could possibly hear from people who visited there and read from media sources mentioning the resort.

Hedonism II (or Hedo 2, or simply Hedo) and its younger sister Hedonism III (or Hedo 3) are similar by their status, type, and amenities. Both are not, *per se*, swing resorts. They are rather clothing-optional ones. Nevertheless, both are friendly and loyal to Lifestyle activities and, therefore, attract swingers like no other place in the world.

The authors have never been to Hedonism III. Yet, we have traveled to Hedonism II 10 times and already booked our 11th getaway.

Long ago, when we were first researching Hedo, we noticed all the reviews coming from resort visitors were just of two types. One group of people was shocked and embarrassed by their Hedo vacationing experience while the other was fully overwhelmed with excitement and enthusiastic about their next visit there. There were no reviews in the middle. Nobody demonstrated indifference. There were virtually no reactions being just okay or so-so type, they all evaluated Hedo as either terrible or excellent. This situation made us somewhat frightened and, at the same time, intrigued. To remind you, we were not swingers in those days. However, our curiosity won and we decided to go there and see for ourselves. As it came out, that was one of the most important decisions of our lives.

Being in our current state, we understand the diametrically irreconcilable reviews. It's simple: a given person's response to a Hedo vacation depends on his or her state of mind and personal expectations.

To illustrate this statement, let's review a discussion that took place on our Web group:

LittleCow222:

We need an advice. We would like to go to some resort—Hedo 2, Hedo 3, or something similar. Would you please give us a tip what would be better for us?

Administrators:

It is hard to say, not knowing what you are looking for.

LittleCow222:

Well, we've been to Sandals recently and liked it. There were great rooms and service, food and drinks were good, too. Sure, we would want to keep those parts unchanged. The only thing we missed is our intimacy boost: we would gladly add some sexual entertainment and open activities to the menu.

Administrators:

Based on your priorities, you would like neither Hedo 2 nor Hedo 3. Food is much worse than a cheap Dominican resort provides; room condition and interior are incomparable with Sandals. Forget about luxury at all! If you need a perfect beach, that's also not there. Besides, most of the times you have to be naked if you want your money to work. Hedo 2 and Hedo 3 have several differences between them, but both are best for Lifestyle-oriented people who are not looking for comfort and luxury, but just for a friendly environment, hot entertainment, and recreational sex. The only thing you would probably like is the drink choice. They serve virtually everything from nice wines to expensive cognacs. Yet, if sex itself and sex-related fun and activities are less important to you than luxury, do not go there, you will be disappointed!

Yes, rooms at Hedo are somewhat outdated, furniture and bathroom fixtures could use some repairs and renovation, and service staff is slow sometimes (*No problem, mon!*). Food selection is far from excellent as well. Both Hedo's beaches are man-made. The prude beach, actually, is not bad at all, while the nude one (and that's where the entire resort crowd usually gathers on swingers' weeks!) sure isn't the best in Caribbean. The sea is shallow, sand is hard-packed and gritty, and there are many different kinds of seaweeds and sea urchins, making the use of swimming shoes a necessity.

However, what is the point in having a luxury room if you are there just four to five hours a day while trying to have a short nap between your steamy activities? What could the perfect food add to your excitement if you have neither time, no desire to eat for the sake of eating? All you actually do is *refuel* yourselves to get enough strength for the next round of fun. As for the seashore issue, we were happy to learn that the perfect beach is not where you are taking sun and sea baths, but rather where you are able to participate in wild adult games and literally have sex with others.

If you appreciate open sexual action, if you prefer Lifestyle-related fun to luxury accommodations, then Hedo is the place to be. You must visit there before you die! You owe it to yourselves.

Vacationing at Hedo always provides us with once-in-a-lifetime experiences, and there is nothing more exciting than getting off the airport shuttle and accepting another "Welcome home!" from the resort's bellboys. In fact, we start smiling from the moment we are landing at the Montego Bay airport, and these wide smiles accompany us until our departure back to reality.

You'll be surprised, but being obsessed with Hedo and, therefore, visiting there multiple times is rather ordinary among swingers. It is usual to meet people who have visited there 20, 30, and even more times. We know a gentleman who vacationed there 49 times!

Simply because you would not want to travel to any other place in the world after you've been to Hedo once, assuming you are a real swinger!

Hedo is more than an all-inclusive resort and another fun-in-the-sun place. Yes, it offers several valuable additions to ordinary all-inclusive packages, such as free tennis courts, free water skiing, free snorkeling, and even free scuba diving. Still, these activities are not the main part of the deal this resort offers. Its pledge to persuade your mind, body, spirit, and soul is not just a nice phrase; it's a day-to-day reality.

Formally, Hedo consists of two parts: *nude* and *prude*. The nude part is clothing optional, while prude suggests no complete nudity (but who cares?). There are two beaches. The prude beach is just an ordinary Caribbean beach; however, the nude one *obligates* you to be naked or else the resort's clothing police will ask you to leave. Males must be fully undressed while females can still wear their bottom pieces, but not the top ones. Not many ladies use this exemption, though. If some lady wears the bottom portion of the swimsuit, it would mean she is having one of her critical days rather than she is shy.

The list of attributes you will find nowhere else but at Hedo is long. There is sexually oriented entertainment and shows presented by the great entertainment team. There is a water slide, which is the largest in the world where complete nudity is perfectly okay. Expect different theme parties every night, including famous Pyjama (Jamaica was part of Britain, thus the spelling) and Toga nights. Join pole-dancing and dirty-dancing contests at the disco. Acknowledge that a baby grand in the piano bar serves as a stage for striptease sessions almost as often as for its original function. Finally, enjoy the nude side's hot tub filled with naked bodies throughout the night into the morning.

The major (and what a huge!) difference from other resorts, however, is the people Hedo attracts! This crowd factor depends on the time of the year, to be exact, on the *week* of the year. If you are visiting Hedo on some non-swingers' week, you likely won't see much action.

Our friends Ben and Paula have never been to Hedo but were eager to try. Once, they called to tell us they got a good deal from their travel agency and were excited about visiting the place for less than half the price we usually pay for our regular second week of January. We warned them the week they intended to book was not a Lifestyle one, and they were at risk of not getting a great deal of fun. Yet, they accepted the deal anyway. The following is their e-mail they sent to us after their vacation took place. They were disappointed.

"We have to agree with you guys, we went to Hedo the last week in February, and it was dead. We tried to approach a few couples, but no fun in the sun. You are right: it is all about when you go. We still had a good time enjoying the naked freedom. But that was basically all."

When it comes to vacationing at Hedo, it is not the only location matters; it is the right timing, too. There are traditional, historically established swingers' take-over weeks. Most popular are Lifestyle weeks in March ("Miss No-Swim-Suit Contest" finals were held on this week for last several years), July (Independence Day Swingers' Parade is a must-see), and mid-October. In addition, the entire month of January is specially designated Hedo Lifestyle month. Yet, the first and fourth weeks of January are less thrilling.

No doubt, the most admired and vastly attended swingers' weeks (and the most expensive ones as well) are the second and the third weeks of January. That's when the resort drops all its restrictions related to nudity as well as to sexual activities on the prude side and the whole place becomes a real swingers' paradise. Not everyone around is a swinger even on those weeks; still, the majority are Lifestyle people, and they rule and rock!

Many Lifestylers from all over the world visit the resort on the same week(s) every year, making Hedo an international Lifestyle reunion scene and adding one more reason to travel there.

Hedo's theme parties are something you will talk about for months after. All those shockingly revealing and shameless outfits challenging each other are also witty and up to the theme. In some cases, the Lifestylers bring these costumes while intending them just for one-time use, for that particular Hedo visit only. People feel comfortable wearing them here but probably would not do so at any other place in the world.

It would take long to describe every activity associated with a Hedo vacation. The authors do not see their goal in filling the blanks here. We would rather like to stress the uniqueness of the Hedo's emotional climate and familiarize you, at least briefly, with the true Hedo spirit.

The following is an excerpt from our Hedo friends' e-mail that gets the job done despite its grammar.

Things we hope/expect to see/hear/do/ experience on the second week of January

Resort at full capacity, staff at full intensity, and lots of stories about how someone's reservations were screwed up and how they were bounced to another resort.

Hearing about the repeaters party and knowing that in 2037 we will have a chance to win a free trip.

Standard question number one, "How late did you stay up last night?"

Hearing someone say the food is good and wondering what they eat the rest of the year.

The Sandals tour boat pulling up close to get a view of the zoo.

Getting a rare chance to see an endangered species: pussy hair.

"Red, Red Wine, twenty each" (all year long when we hear one of the songs from the Hedo loop out in public we both just smile at each other).

Adventures of the nude Catamaran cruise. Rasta Ralphie, Rick's tourista trappa, etc.

What celebrity look-alikes will we have this year? Last year: Bruce Willis, Newt Gingrich. Previous year we had Eric Clapton and Tommy Lee.

Playing the "so which one do you think is the wife?" game.

When the guy lights up his cigar in the hot tub, 30 people at once hold him underwater until he gets the hint.

Getting the answer to the question "Is my dick average?"

Ongoing updates of who went to Desire during the last year (and why they are back at Hedo 2).

How we got into the Lifestyle. Always an interesting subject.

How I got drunk yesterday. Always an uninteresting subject (except to the drinker).

Hot tub usuals: Too hot, too cold, too much "floaties," just right!

The look of the newbies when they see their first PDA and try to figure out how to look without looking.

The look of the newbies when they do their first PDA and try to figure out how to be seen without being seen.

Finding a rock with someone's name you recognize, and now you have the answer to the "which one is the wife" question.

Having the chance to ask, "Just how well does that genital piercing work?"

Watching people trying to figure out how to keep it in while screwing on a raft.

Noticing how much less comfortable the beautiful young things are with their perfect bodies than us old farts in our wrinkled suits.

The smiling faces of the Canada gang. These people may be from the frozen north, but they know how to warm the place up.

Three-D porn, live and in person (or persons).

Swinging from A to Z

The great imponderables: Who will you be with today? Did you have hot water yesterday? Is it true that jerk chicken makes you horny and prolongs erections?

Hearing, after you answer standard question number one above: "Oh yeah? You went to bed at 5 a.m.? Well, just after that the really wild shit went down!"

Hedo vs. Desire
By Larry

This is about measuring similar things differently.

What is better, Hedo or Desire? This question is probably one of the most frequently asked in the Lifestyle. Stories comparing these two resorts are popular among swingers.

Desire is also a clothing-optional and Lifestyle-friendly resort, situated on the Riviera Maya, 20 minutes from the Cancun International Airport.

While Hedo welcomes both couples and singles, Desire is an exclusively couples' resort.

There are plenty of different reviews comparing these two resorts. Some prefer Hedo to Desire; some have the opposite view. These resorts are competitors, and each has its own view of reaching its goals.

After being at Hedo five times (and hearing good and bad fairy tales about Desire), we decided to check out Desire. Being experienced, we did a little research and joined a group of Texas swingers on the week they took over the resort.

The following is our getaway's review we've placed on our Web group:

DESIRE, CANCUN, MEXICO

We are back from the resort we have heard many different things about. We were there with two our closest friends-couples. One of these couples is a member of this very group, Pete and Kari from Toronto, Canada.

We finally decided to sacrifice our regular Hedo week and check out Desire instead.

Where do we begin?

Rooms and general service are A++, food quality and selection is great. Even the assortment of drinks is almost as good as at Hedo (a nice surprise).

At first sight, the resort itself caters to people like us. All the beds with sheets and cushions around the pool and on the beach make you think you are welcome to use them appropriately right away. That's exactly what we did the first minute all six of us met.

However, the resort's personnel stopped us, "No open sexual activities at the pool!" We moved to the beach. Same story. We moved to the main bar area, and with the same outcome. One of us asked, "May I at least touch myself?" The answer was, "Not in a sexual way."

Desire only allows open recreational sex in designated areas: near the hot tub and at the disco's playroom. We checked out both regularly but didn't see anything happening.

The resort was virtually empty at 1 a.m., the time when fun just starts at Hedo. All the activities, if any, were taking place in the privacy of the rooms. We hardly believed this quiet time was happening on a swingers' takeover week!

The quality of the daytime entertainment was poor, and, frankly, all the ball throwing, splash making, and rings-on-bottle targeting contests were more suitable for nursing homes and were not even comparable with those at Hedo.

The nighttime entertainment was good and we enjoyed fun contests at the disco, though. One of us (guess who?) was successful in the striptease contest and won a prize.

The music broadcast in the morning at the pool (relaxation-oriental-classic-cosmic-electronic-freaking mix) made us feel we were at a funeral. We called this music "anti-erection therapy." We complained several times, but nothing changed.

Finally, after construction started just outside our friends' rooms, we went to the reception desk and asked where did they expect us to have daytime sex if it was strictly forbidden all-around the resort and now we could not use two out of three of our rooms due to the noise? We forced management to give us an additional free room for sexual activities. We happily used this room for group parties during the last two days as a hospitality suite.

The good part is we made new friends (some are the newest members of this group) and managed to have fun. The blowjob and pussy-eating contests involving up to eight couples were a huge success, and some group orgies were not bad at all.

We thank our friends Kari and Pete for their huge effort and contribution to the fun. In fact, Kari performed the entire PR and organization functions for our little group, or "the family," as some of our new friends called us.

We do not regret visiting Desire. Our time was not bad at all. Still, we'll never return there and rather will stick to Hedo on future getaways. We are not looking for great service and perfect food. Open sex and sex-related fun are more important to us.

Swing conventions

By Larry and Mia

The sky is the only limit.

Lifestyle conventions are the hottest swingers' events you can be part of. Swingers from all over the world attend and enjoy them repeatedly.

Numerous swingers' groups and organizations host their conventions throughout the year and throughout the world. Conventions are a perfect way of meeting other like-minded people and make new Lifestyle friends. Besides, they create a great opportunity to explore various erotic and sexual activities you may not experience while at local swing clubs, parties, or even swing resorts.

Unexpectedly, conventions are also a great place to attend for Lifestyle newbies and less-experienced couples because their educational aspects are one of the best ways to learn about every attribute of swinging, including rules and etiquette, types and common activities, safety and STDs, and more. Attending conventions greatly helps expand sexuality in a safe, informative environment.

As a rule, conventions take over the hotels that cater for the whole convention time exclusively to attendees. No matter, if the given convention accommodates more than a thousand swingers or just a little over a hundred, all the conventions are *closed* events. They do not allow strangers in.

Usually, conventions go on for four to five days with Wednesday or Thursday as an arrival day and Sunday for departure.

At a typical swing convention you would enjoy themed dance parties and after-parties, pole dancing and striptease competitions, naked pool festivities, various workshops, Ms. & Mr. Convention contests, a choice of seminars, fashion shows, concerts, sexual merchandise vendors, erotic art and photo exhibits, parades, and, of course, sex—lots of it.

A significant part of the fun only found at conventions is specially designated hospitality suites. Most conventions provide an array of them, set up by theme or type of sexual activity, such as Bi-Women room, Salsa room, Dungeon (BDSM equipped), Sensual Massage room, Dark room, Black Light room, Chocolate room, and Swing room (outfitted with swings). Often, conventions reserve the whole hotel floor for their play activities, and every single room on that floor becomes a hospitality suite.

Below is the post on the Web group relating to our most recent convention visit:

> We are back from [*****] convention.
> This convention was maybe the smallest by attendance among all we have visited so far, yet it was beautifully organized.

Swinging from A to Z

The hosts situated their event at a nice all-suite hotel with a heated pool that became clothing-optional. They also included breakfast and lunch in the package.

There were three fun theme nights with incredible costumes, contests, prizes, including three free nights at Hedo, etc. There also were some seminars and workshops, as usual.

The true highlight of the event, though, was the so-called "Red Light District" set on the first floor of one of the hotel's buildings. It included about a dozen of one-bedroom suites. To name a few, there were Dark Room, Swing Room (you know, the swings that make you "swing"), Snack Room, Dungeon (for BDSM people), Sensitive Massage Room, Couples-Only Room, Sybian Room (with that scary mechanical thing some ladies enjoy), and Blowjob Room (nice screen with holes for three men at a time). What was the best in our view, though, was a Chocolate Room. Yes, they served many different chocolates there, but main part was six well-endowed black gentlemen ready to fulfill every fantasy of any lady who dares.

Overall, we had a lot of fun, made new friends from all over the U.S. and seriously consider going back for more in the future.

The authors do not intend to promote any particular convention, exactly as it was with swing Web sites. If you are interested, make your Web search for "swing conventions" or "Lifestyle conventions." You will find most of them listed.

Approaching at resorts and conventions
By Larry and Mia

Here is one more nuance.

The technique of approaching others while you are at a resort or convention is different from the one at other Lifestyle events. People come to the club or party just for a few hours, while at a convention or resort they intend to stay several days. The relaxing atmosphere of this unique *vanilla-free* environment makes a difference in everyone's mindset.

Swingers are still determined to engage in as many sexual encounters as possible. Yet, they have to spread their time between different activities for them to taste at least a little of everything. There are too many actions going on at the same time, making deciding what to do at each moment more difficult.

Hence, scheduled dates do not necessarily work here because either you or your partners-to-be could be *on the fly* involved in some unanticipated act. Thus, you could easily miss the appointment.

The key word for appropriate understanding the situation is *spontaneous*. Yes, you behave more impulsively and unprompted while you are at a resort or convention. Spur of the moment often decides for you.

The following is from a discussion on our Web group:

KARI&PETE:

Kari and I are going to Niagara Falls, Canada, for a Valentine's Day swing convention in February. We don't know anyone there, but we have learned how not to waste time on people with hang-ups. Mia and Larry have been our inspiration. We ask couples about their Lifestyle choices right after meeting them.

"Do you want?" If the answer is "No," then we move on! My friends, time is running out, and we want to have lots of sex. Therefore, we have found no matter where we are playing, being completely open and honest is the best policy.

ADMINISTRATORS:

This might be not easy to do for the first time, but once you do it, it goes smoothly enough.

When you are at a convention or other similar setting (Hedo, Desire etc.) the steps leading to total exclusion of time waste are:

1. Spot the couple you like.

2. Approach them immediately and ask if they want to play with you.

3. If their answer is "Yes," grab them instantly (scheduled for later dates often will not work) and take them to your room. If the answer is "No," or any other variation of "No" (like "We'll tell you later," "We need to get to know you better," etc.), go to step one above.

Never wait in line and never hesitate. Be active. This way we always get what we want in desired quality and quantities.

Kisses to all, Larry & Mia

Another major difference is that at conventions and resorts people you would like to play with are often part of some group. Maybe three or four (or more) couples of their friends are always with them, making them seem unapproachable. Sometimes, such a group looks self-sufficient and ready to reject anyone trying to break in. Not true! Swingers are always ready for new contacts and always desire them. The more the merrier!

The following story illustrates the statement above. During a Hedo vacation while the lunchtime games took place in the main dining area, we picked up some food and took seats at a large table next to an attractive couple in their late 30s. (We always try to make new contacts during mealtime. Don't ever try to find a secluded spot just for you two. Always sit next to new people. They might be fun and, who knows, may be more than just fun!)

Our tablemates were sad because they were leaving in an hour and waiting for their airport shuttle. We started a conversation. You know, the usual—where are you from, what are your names, how did you like it here, how many times were you here before, etc. The Canadians (they were from Vancouver) visited Hedo for the first time, liked the resort, but told us they expected more from the sexual part of their getaway.

They said, "We might be too selective, but we've only spotted three couples here whom we would like to play with, and you were one of them." We were pleased and asked why they did not invite us over because we would gladly do so! Their reaction was, "Really? But you were always in the middle of the group of friends. We did not expect you to have fun with someone outside of your group. You looked like you were extremely busy, and it just did not make sense to even try to approach you!"

We immediately invited the Canadians to our room (another our Hedo rule: book a room as close to the main dining area as possible) and had an amazing quickie. How much more fun all of us could have had if they approached us the minute they decided they liked us?

Chapter 8

Your Look

What to wear in the Lifestyle
By Mia

> *Brevity is the soul of lingerie.*
> *—Dorothy Parker*

It is critical to look exceptional.

Your swinging outfit matters. People do judge you by what you wear. Besides, it affects your overall performance.

In the Lifestyle, your look is even more important than in the vanilla world. Clothes, shoes, and accessories you are wearing result in successful continuation of your first contact and the whole outcome of your acquaintance with new people. Ideally, you should look stylish, contemporary, and as young as possible.

A smart approach to your clothes selection is your key to success. The parts of that success are:
- Getting the attention of everyone around.
- Putting yourself in a good mood.
- Allowing yourself to have a fun time.
- Making new friends.

Remember, even if you have an ideal body, beautiful face, great hair, and are confident, your matching outfit is still a huge plus. Therefore, be careful with what you wear. The choice must be right for your body and should reflect your preferences.

Before your wardrobe has enough to choose from, you have to fill it up. The whole process of buying a new piece of clothing is complicated. Concentrate on your body-specific requirements. Cover up the negatives of your physique (unfortunately, almost all of us have them) and draw attention to positives (fortunately, we all know what they are). Simply put, camouflage your bad parts while exposing the good ones.

Search the Web for "sexy costumes," "sexy dresses," and "sexy club wear." Just don't miss the word "sexy" since it defines what you are looking for. Your swing website could also provide you with some useful links. Or go to some store that sells *young* party clothes.

At swingers' events you should look about the same way as you would want to look at a dance club, just more sluttish.

Basic tips for gentlemen

No:
- Formal suit, formal shirt with tie (forget about ties forever!).
- Sports wear.
- Shorts (even if you are at resort's party and the weather is hot, long pants are better).
- Sneakers.

Yes:
- Well-fit fashionable slacks or jeans ("well-fit" is the key).
- Sport coat (young looking).
- Dressy shirt, printed or with some embroidery, pleats, nice buttons. Always wear your shirt *over* the pants. This approach would make you look younger and up-to-date.
- T-shirt might be acceptable if you have some real gym achievements to demonstrate.
- Stylish contemporary shoes, not necessarily impressive, but never of the Birkenstock style.

Before you are leaving for a party, always ask your wife or girlfriend what she thinks about your look. If she likes it, that means you appear fine, better than usual, and she will enjoy your company. Consequently, you've improved your chance that other women will like you, so you have achieved your goal.

Most likely, you already have everything necessary in your possession and don't need to buy a lot of additional items. Just combine all the parts, your clothes and your shoes well.

Guys, if you did not pay attention before, now is the right time. You will score positive glances and approving smiles. Perhaps, you may even hear some compliments.

Basic tips for ladies

Disappointing news for you, girls: unlike your partners, you will need to buy new clothes.

To save your money, bear in mind you need to acquire extremely sexy items that should be only suitable for swingers' events. The check-up condition should be as follows: if you could put on the particular dress or shoes at a vanilla party, they will most likely be unacceptable for a swingers' event. It would be even better if you could buy *shockingly* sexy things rather than just sexy! Do not be afraid to look exceptional, the Lifestyle is all about it.

No:
- Clothes you use at the office.
- Clothes you could walk the streets in.
- Your ordinary vanilla cocktail dress (even if it is open enough).
- Comfortable shoes.

Yes:
- Short dress or a set of small top and mini skirt, no sleeves ever!
- Slim pants, cat suit, hot shorts, or rompers.
- Corsets, lingerie (as your top attire).
- Accessories: sexy jewelry (not necessarily expensive), belts, hats, gloves, wigs (you will be surprised how a wig can change your personality).
- Shoes or boots on 4"- to 7"-high heel or platform (inevitable!).

High heels do miracles! On the one hand, they increase your height and make your legs appear longer. On the other, they improve your posture without any additional exercise and training.

Pay attention to colors. You should prefer bright and exotic ones. In the vanilla world, you might favor classic colors such as black, brown, and dark blue. Forget about vanilla standards. Even if you are not at tropical resort, but rather at your native city, employ sultry blush anyway. Electric blue, hot pink, astonishing red and crazy yellow should be your first choices. Color affects everyone's perception. Use colors that flatter you.

You don't have to present your whole outfit in bright colors, yet you should make some color accents at any part of it—just the top or the shoes, or bold jewelry, or a hat, or gloves. Don't forget to add some color and shine to your makeup as well. Make it extraordinary, kinky, and dramatically different from what you usually wear in the vanilla world.

You don't have to buy lots of new clothes at once. Try two or three new outfits to begin with. You need to make sure your choice is correct, consistent with your own style, and fits your main purpose—attending those *special* events.

Can you say, "This one is a real slut and no man can resist her!" after looking at the mirror? Does your husband shout, "Wow! I want this woman right now, right here!" after looking at you once you are ready to leave for the party? Good!

Your attire at a theme party
By Mia

Reveal your creativity and imagination!

As a rule, most of the parties you will attend will have themes. Some themed swingers' get-togethers will have an entertainment and other activities devoted to a particular theme. Others will not have them. Regardless, the theme is always all about what the hosts expect you to wear.

Usually, the hosts announce the theme for an upcoming event as far in advance as possible. So, if you were invited, you would have enough time to prepare.

Most popular themes include Pajama, Toga, and Lace & Leather. However, depending on the hosts' creativity, the theme could be anything. Some examples of themed events the authors of this book recently visited or hosted themselves are "Black & White," "Tropical," "The Lesser the Better," "Medieval," "Hocus-Pocus," "Roman Orgy," and "Spark & Glitter."

Sometimes, the hosts insist their guests' outfits should be consistent with the particular theme. They even promise to limit access to their event exclusively to guests who are dressed appropriately. In this case, you must cooperate to attend.

More often, the hosts' theme requirements are optional, and you will be able to make a decision yourselves. However, it is an exciting feeling to be a part of specially dressed crowd. It will give you an opportunity to integrate with the crowd from the minute you enter the door.

Discussing each other's costumes and the entire aspects of your research and preparations related to them is a perfect subject for an initial chat and breaking the ice with others. Besides, supporting the given theme can make your involvement in an event exceptional and provide your best memories ever. Wearing remarkable costumes makes you feel unusual by adding extra exhilaration to every moment of your participation. Moreover, your pictures, if allowed to take them (and if it will be possible to show them due to their content), will make a perfect addition to your Lifestyle photo album.

Wearing a particular costume and impersonating someone (or something) could satisfy your life partner's unfulfilled sexual fantasies and might be an added surprise for you. While discussing your possible outfits for some themed party you've been invited to, you might hear from your husband he has always dreamed of seeing you in the attire of a classic Playboy Bunny at the Easter party.

In return, he might be pleased to learn that you prefer him to escort you to the Halloween event as a Police Officer or Firefighter.

Swinging from A to Z

For that reason, do not hesitate to talk about your outfit options and do not disconnect yourselves from additional fun opportunities. Again, fun is the reason you are in the Lifestyle. Try to get as much of it as possible!

You don't need to have a complete set of clothing to support a particular theme. You can achieve the required stylish look by adding some accessories to your existing sexy outfit. For instance, an eye patch, clip in the ear, and bandanna would make you a Pirate. Little plaits with bright bows and short white socks would create a Schoolgirl, and a 99 cents plastic star could turn you into a Sheriff.

It does not matter what particular details you concentrate on. What matters is:

- You should look (and feel!) attractive.
- You should appear as exceptional within the theme as possible.
- You should be comfortable and confident in your attire.
- You should be proud of your outfit.
- You must love yourself in that particular image.

A couple of years ago we hosted a Black Tie party. We did not ask for formal traditional black tie attire. All we requested from our guests were any kind of ties or bows each worn the way they would like to and at any place they would find appropriate.

We established the prize for the best outfit. Additionally, the winner acquired an official title "Irresistible Person." (Part of our entertainment that time was my "Dancing Tie" performance. I was dancing while moving a large golden bow tie all over my body.)

After everyone arrived, we saw quite a wide range of outfits: from a genuine Armani tuxedo with bow tie over the snow-white formal shirt to open sluttish little dresses with large and little black bows over the arms or legs of their possessors. As it turned out, though, the winner was the gentleman who, on the first sight, did not have the tie at all. He told everyone he *had* the tie on, but would show it later. Finally, he presented it. Undoubtedly, a tie *there* looked exceptionally original, intelligent, and inviting! Our jury panel selected from the crowd could not resist but declare him a winner. As a result, the guy was a center of attention all night (and all morning).

Sharp, non-standard ideas can achieve the desired result in a most efficient way without significant expense.

Your clothes at resorts
By Mia

> *Sex is a bad thing because it rumples the clothes.*
> —Jackie Onassis

Making a fashion statement...

Deliberations on party costumes are, doubtlessly, the most popular at Lifestyle resorts. Morning talks of that kind are mostly about who was wearing what yesterday. Evening ones are about what will they wear tonight. At the beach or at the pool, it's common to hear questions like, "What color costume will you wear?" or "Where did you buy and how much did you pay for those shoes?" Often a gentleman warns everyone to make sure they pay attention to his wife's outfit tonight since it will be exotic.

If you are vacationing at such a resort, the rule is to bring lots of dresses, shoes, and accessories. You should have at least one outfit per night. However, do not be surprised if some people change costumes several times an evening. It is common to see arriving couples who have three, four, or even more suitcases with them. Of course, it depends on how large or small their costumes are. We fit everything we need into one suitcase.

You should check in advance the themes for each night of your stay and plan accordingly. The easiest way to get this information is the resort's website. This way, you will be able to see the resorts' general themes. For instance, traditional Hedo themes are Toga, PJ (Pyjama and Lingerie), Western, International, Oldies, Pirates, Mardi Gras, and Reggae.

If you are traveling as a part of a swingers' group, your group could arrange special themes or modify the existing ones. For instance, your group's hosts could transform a general Toga Night into a Purple Toga Night. Instead of an Oldies theme, your group could use a School Girls and Teachers. Consult the host couple of your group for additional information. If you book with the particular group, you will have the host couple's contact information well before your departure.

It is not obligatory to support every theme, and no one will expect it from you. You are more than welcome to improvise. Just make sure your outfits are dramatically different from one another. However, and I repeat, it is preferable to have more than one per night.

I take with me about 20 outfits for a one-week stay. Of course, Larry doesn't need that many. One per night is enough for men.

On our second Hedo getaway, I announced to our friends that I would change my outfits each time after having sex. Soon, half the resort was watching me, with widespread enthusiasm and congratulations after each costume change. On the other hand, if I did not change for a relatively long time, everyone around was concerned. Why am I still wearing the same dress for the last two hours? Did I run out of new outfits? Am I tired, or (God forbid!) don't I want to have sex anymore? It became a little tradition since, and I hear similar questions, condolences, and congratulations every time we are at the resort.

I always bring three or four different wigs with me. I can be a long-haired blonde now and a stylish brunette with a short haircut 15 minutes later. Like nothing else, wigs dramatically change your appearance and even personality. Sometimes, people recognize me just because Larry accompanies me. At times, I have to introduce myself twice to the same person during the same night!

One of the common activities at resorts (as well as at swing conventions) is a contest for the best Dirty T-Shirts. The whole idea here is about amusing, witty, and entertaining sex-related text printed on a t-shirt and matching this text to your personality. You can buy those shirts at specialty stores as well as on the Web. They can be expensive.

While preparing for our Desire vacation (this t-shirt theme was among our group's), we made custom t-shirts. We visited there with friends and bought four plain white t-shirts for $1 each at a convenience store. We cut two of these shirts (intended for girls) to make them shorter and made a few cutouts on them. Using color markers, we wrote the following. For guys: "Your room or mine?" and "Only two women short of a threesome!" For girls: "Proven penis enlarger" and "I am not cheap, but I am on sale this week."

Our t-shirts, being custom-made, were somewhat out of the ordinary, and many people asked us where we bought them. Some of these people became our play-partners. For us it is a technical matter to convince an attractive couple to have mutual fun after they demonstrated their interest. Our unusual t-shirts were the reason for that initial curiosity.

Bear in mind, the inquisitiveness your unique and unusual outfit generates in people around often leads to your general success and added thrill. Again and again, you can achieve this goal for less while using your creativeness.

Chapter 9

Sex

Group play and orgies
By Larry and Mia

> Is sex dirty? Only if it's done right.
> —Woody Allen

Here it comes, the top of the line.

Group sex is an activity with more than two couples involved. Actually, you can observe group play or participate in one at any swing club or swing party. If, for instance, three couples are having sex in the same room (not talking about the same bed), this activity is by definition a group play. Even if these couples do not exchange partners, it is still a group.

What happens if they do exchange partners? Will it become an orgy? The answer is, "Possibly but not necessarily!"

Our parties are orgies, and the following is our playgroup's profile on one of the swing websites where we advertise our sessions:

ISO attractive and intelligent, hard-core orgy-ready swingers

We are looking for:

Intelligent and attractive full-swap swingers for group hard-core orgies.

All of us know: couple-to-couple play is somewhat complicated. In 99% of the cases, one has to "do it for the team," but that doesn't happen at our settings. Everyone plays with everyone he/she likes (of course, mutual click is necessary as everywhere in the Lifestyle).

In other words, you will be a valuable addition to our playgroup if you are able to leave your relationship at the entry door and have fun as independent single swingers, which defines an orgy.

Description:

We are seasoned swingers having numerous like-minded friends—swinging couples and singles of both genders, and of ages from their 20s to 40s. Our get-togethers are dedicated to the Lifestyle and are completely free-of-charge events.

To apply for an invitation, you should be:

- Intelligent and friendly.
- Reliable and discreet.
- Attractive and fit.
- Drama-free, full swap, and ready for group action.
- Couples not older than 45, singles not older than 40, and we mean your real age, not what you state in your profile.

Additional requirements for single guys only:

- Tall and well built, 6 feet tall, 200 pounds at least.
- At least 8" endowed. Thick is a plus.
- With great stamina and able to perform in the group scene.

If you believe the orgy is the same as one-on-one play, you are wrong. Often, experienced guys cannot get it up at our parties.

If you think some lady may choose to stimulate you rather than play with a gentleman who does not need any stimulation, you are wrong again.

Gentlemen, if you do not fit into the above standards, you won't get enough attention at our settings compared to our existing single friends. It happened before.

An orgy is all about person-to-person play. Assume the following situation: three couples are in one room: M1 and F1, M2 and F2, and M3 and F3. Presumably, M1 and F2 would love to play together while F1 does not like M2. In this case, a M1 and F1 combination with M2 and F2 is hardly possible. However, if F1 is okay with M3 and F3 is just fine with M2, we have a situation where everyone will be happy.

A true orgy is group play free of couple-to-couple associations, where everyone behaves as a single swinger. At the orgy, you do not have to share your partner with someone in particular. You simply share him/her with *any person* he/she prefers to play with. Hence, more opportunities exist for every participant.

If you had two or three contacts at the club or a non-orgy private party, consider yourselves successful. If you had less than six to eight at the orgy with 10 to 12 couples, it was bad luck. At orgies with perfectly selected attendees, the number of your sexual encounters will be a function of your energy resources. At our parties, for instance, every gentleman plays with virtually every lady.

Orgies are not for everyone. They require the highest level of trust within inner couples' relationships and extensive Lifestyle background. You should be able to approve your loved one's behavior *beforehand* and always feel comfortable, no matter who both of you play with at a given moment. You should be ready to arrive to the party and to depart after one as a couple, but to perform as two self-sufficient persons during the session.

Below is some of the feedback that our friends left on the above website profile. The authors suggest it could be useful for you to look at real swingers' responses to real swingers' events, and consider what they appreciate most.

> Were we in heaven? Amazing hosts, classy and hot couples, comfortable and relaxing atmosphere. These people are what they say on the profile and more! We've had a night filled with engaging conversations, witty humor, and lusty synergy. We can't wait for the next party!

*

If you are looking to fulfill a fantasy or if you just want an amazing, sexy night, do not hesitate to contact this group. The honest and respectful way of planning our meeting put us at ease right away and led to an incredibly wet and wild night of intense pleasure! Thank you for the classy and naughty adventure!

*

We love those parties and always look forward to the next one. The settings are perfect. The hosts have the best crowd, with a great combination of old friends and new faces, not to mention the play area is convenient and well-equipped. We have the great times at those parties.

*

These are amazing parties! The guests are always 100% full swap and ready to go. It's hard to put into words how awesome it is to attend a real swing orgy. If you get a chance to join this group, I highly recommend you do so.

*

Just imagine a beautiful home filled with hot, sexy people. Well-endowed handsome men, titillating, enthralling, exotic beauties, couples who can hold an intellectual conversation, and gracious hosts who go out of their way to accommodate each and every guest. They honored us by inviting to their events. We look forward with great anticipation to our next four-hour drive; it's just so worth it! If you are privileged enough to be invited, drop your other plans and find out just how great your sex life can be.

*

They throw amazing parties! They are warm and friendly hosts who know how to put together a good party and make everyone (even new people) feel welcome. Everyone who attends is sexy, fun, and great to know. We make it a point not to miss their events. If you were lucky to get an invitation, please attend!

*

We have been lucky to visit their parties twice and cannot wait for the next gathering. These two are extremely fun, welcoming, super sexy, and host the best parties we have ever been to or even heard about (we drive more than four hours to be part of it). They have only quality, sexy, fun, classy people in their home who know how to make their party experience flow with sensuality at a comfort level that makes all feel special and privileged to attend. There are a lot of good humor, intellectual conversations, and unbelievable sex! Do not pass up a party invite from them. You will be talking about the visuals and fun times for months on end.

We always tell our first-timers, "This closet on your right is for your relationship. Stick it there and don't worry, it will be perfectly safe. Just don't forget to pick it up on your way home!"

Bisexuality and the Lifestyle
By Mia

> *Bisexuality immediately doubles your chances for a date on Saturday night.*
> —Rodney Dangerfield

> *The Catholic Church doesn't recognize homosexuals— that's funny, I always can.*
> —Patty Rosborough

Female bisexuality is native to the Lifestyle. If you have a profile on any swing website, you've noticed a majority of ladies present themselves as bi, bi-curious, or at least bi-friendly—about 90% of them.

However, men advertising themselves as bi are rare. The majority of men are homophobic. Many prefer to underline their heterosexuality to exclude the slightest doubts even before they agree to meet other couples. If a gentleman openly announces his bisexuality (or even bi-curiosity), he objectively reduces his own and, therefore, his wife's chances of matching with couples where the males are straight. The odds for him and his better half go down even if he promises to keep his distance from men and only play with women.

The Lifestyle is not free of double standards, too. The bias against men's bisexuality proves it. As for the authors of this book, we perfectly accept men's right to be bisexual, yet, since Larry doesn't have any slightest interest in men, we never experimented in this area.

My own bisexuality was one of most important discoveries I've made in the Lifestyle. All my life before entering the swinging world, I never suspected I could be interested in other females. I am sure not a lesbian at all. Sexually, I would never prefer women to men, even the most beautiful ladies over the ugliest gentlemen!

However, girls' play is a delight and makes any sexual experience exceptional. Besides, it amuses (and arouses) everyone around.

Ladies involvement in bisexuality can be of a different type and of a varying intensity:

- Pleasure of watching other women in action.
- Inspiration of bodily contacts with other girls, almost innocent waist and hips embraces, light breast touches.
- Desire of full strength whole body hugs, kisses (mouth, breast, and neck), butt squeezing.
- Explicit sexual play with stimulation of genitalia with hands, tongue (giving or receiving head), and sex toys.

Ladies, if your perceptions and feelings about some woman (not necessarily every one) are any of those, you are nothing but a *bi*. No matter, if you are keeping your distance bi-friendly, or fully involved bisexual, you are bi anyway because you love women. It gives you another way to increase your own pleasure, widen your sensuality, and entertain your partner.

Most of men and women get great pleasure from watching girls play. Even if Larry is somewhat tired of sex and satisfied, he will be full of enthusiasm again the minute I start playing with the other lady.

Many couples choose to begin with female-to-female foreplay before having actual full-swap fun. For their better halves, this foreplay can be active or passive; i.e., some prefer to do the actual job while others just provide their bodies with equal pleasure. Only women know what women want and appreciate most!

Girls' play is one of the best ways to start the action. At one of our house parties we had a ladies' show that involved seven of my bisexual girlfriends and me. We played in one naked group as four female couples using our favorite sex toys without any hesitation. We enjoyed each other while being watched by about 30-person crowd, including our husbands and boyfriends. The show was a success.

Afterward, our playroom became busy at full capacity. We heard a lot of great compliments that night. After more than two years, our friends still ask for a sequel.

Females' bisexuality introduces one more nuance in the Lifestyle. If you intend to play with a couple, learn well in advance how bisexual or how straight this couple's better half is. You can stay completely relaxed if the lady is bi at any level. Conversely, be warned if she is straight. You could expect some negatives to surface while you are with a straight female. Some of them are:

- A straight woman possibly will not be happy to share her partner with another woman who is, in her opinion, more attractive. Sometimes, if this is the case, she will not share at all.
- Even if she agrees to swap partners, there still could be some jealousy.
- You can only be sure everything is fine if a straight woman truly enjoys sex for the sake of it and your partner can satisfy her.

I love women, but I could easily live without girl-to-girl foreplay as long as I am positive we are free of unexpected problems and unpleasant situations. As our swinging experience suggests, it is much easier to deal with couples where the ladies are at least bi-friendly. For us, a huge plus is participating in Lifestyle activities involving bi women. I would say it is not a "Bi+" but rather "A+"!

Does size matter?
By Mia

This is the one of most controversial questions.

People deliberate this matter at all times and in all places endlessly. If you offered this question to me, I would definitely answer, "Yes, it does!" For me, the size always matters, even if I am not sure what kind of size you are talking about and what you are trying to measure. Plain logic and my life experience bring me to this conclusion.

No matter what kind of issue you are trying to resolve, the only response you could trust should come from someone competent. If it now comes to evaluation of men's endowment, you have to ask women who know the subject well and can formulate an objective judgment. Don't ask anyone who does not have this knowledge and who did not have a chance to compare. Ask the swingers instead!

Once we were attending a couples' seminar at Hedo. All the ladies sat in the center of the room and answered their husbands' questions, which were anonymous, on paper. As soon as we ladies received this "Does size matter?" question, there was no hesitation at all. Our common immediate and definite reply was a loud "Yes!" All of us, with no exception, voted for the same! You can trust our combined opinion since every one of us was more or less an experienced swinger at the time.

At any swingers' event, you will notice the special attention women pay to well-endowed gentlemen. There is always a little crowd around them. What's more, there is an added enthusiasm among the female guests when a guy, who is well-known by his astonishing gift, enters the door.

There are two different aspects for women when it comes to playing with hung men.

Psychological

Psychosomatic factors play a leading role in our attention to large penises. Even if a particular woman is able to achieve complete and full satisfaction while playing with an average partner (absolute majority of us do!), the very moment she sees an extra-ordinary penis she feels an extra excitement and an elevated sexual desire.

Physiological

From most of my girlfriends' and my experiences (yes, we share!), and based on women's physical realities and physiological perception, we prefer larger size penises because of their girth rather than length. An excessively long penis can easily hurt. For most of our vaginas, the ideal penis would be somewhat thicker and a little longer than average.

Here is the right place to establish what the average penis size means. If we were to add up the length of every erect adult penis in the world and divide the total by the number of penises, what would that result be? The answer is anywhere from five to six inches, depending on which study you want to rely on. That's right; after dozens of rigorous scientific studies conducted in every part of the world, the only thing I can tell you with certainty is that if man's penis is less than five inches it's smaller than average, and if it's larger than six inches it's bigger than average.

You've heard one of popular answers to the question we discuss: "Size does not matter—it is how to use it." Although I oppose the first part of this statement, I am quick to agree with the second. The art of penis deployment is impossible to underestimate. Consequently, gentlemen who possess a deep knowledge of it are always on the top of my list.

If a situation offers me a choice of two guys to play with: (1) with large penis and lower than average abilities, (2) with average size and above average skills, my choice would be number two. I mean, my *first choice* would be number two. Then, I would gladly use number one just as an exceptional live dildo and not without pleasure.

The right aptitude, creativeness, and impeccable sexual energy always beat a standalone larger-size penis. These qualities literally *add inches to* their vendor (but, again, only if there is already something to add to!)

Just imagine how fantastic your encounter would be with the man who possesses the best lovemaking skills and well endowment at the same time. They are rare and in high demand at any party. A woman who never experienced an encounter with such a man deserves my deepest condolences.

Talking about endowment, there are some prevalent beliefs that *predict* size of the penis based on man's external qualities even before you see him naked.

It is widespread to think the penis is small if:
- Man's fingers are short and thin.
- Man's feet are small.
- Man's nose is small.
- Man is tall ("Tall men are good to go to parade with and only then!").

It is also common to expect a not bad size if all the above is an opposite.

All the above statements are false and misleading. You can't forecast the size of a man's penis until you see it; only trust your eyes!

On a second thought, don't completely trust your eyes, too. If you see a naked man on the nude beach and his gift is limp, it is impossible to say what exactly it turns into if the man gets excited. There are more than enough gentlemen with large penises looking small and somewhat hidden when not erect. Therefore, I would have to rephrase my previous statement. The correct version should read,

"Trust your own eyes, but only after you use your own hands and your own mouth!"

Another common size-related myth is we women would never play with smaller guys after we've had fun with larger ones. This is so not true! A healthy woman could and would enjoy both *regressions* and *progressions,* even during the same play session. Every man is different, and there is always something to enjoy.

Size and skills do matter, but order of sizes and skills does not.

Interracial sexual contacts
By Mia

> *Sex is a lot like pizza. When it's good, it's really good; when it's bad, it's still kinda good.*
> —Brandon Lyon

All of us look for different choices. We could have fond memories of our Italy vacation, but still would prefer our next destination to be Brazil or India. We could prefer Japanese sushi for our favorite dinner entree, yet we might have tried Jamaican jerk chicken and would want to experience its unique taste from time to time.

It is perfectly standard for people to look for exclusive encounters, abnormal situations, and unique perceptions. We enter the Lifestyle with similar hopes, only this time relating to our sexual side. Sometimes, we don't even know for sure what exactly these expectations are all about and have no clue what the hell we need!

Being in the Lifestyle, account for a wide range of activities and make them rather atypical. Accepting interracial sexual contacts is always a right move. Diversity is a native Lifestyle attribute.

If you have not yet had a chance to play with a partner of a different race, you owe it to yourself. It could become a substantial addition to your sexual life, as well as it could reward you with a rich sensual experience. Everyone is different, and, to make sure what you like and dislike, you have to try.

Not every woman can decide on an interracial contact effortlessly. Our men are easier. If they have an opportunity, they often go for it without hesitation. On the other hand, most of us women are more conservative and are not that sensually determined.

One of Larry's fantasies was watching me with a black guy. I had it on my "to-do" list for a long time, but couldn't force myself to make it a reality. Finally, my husband pushed me to make this step.

It was our last day at Hedo. (Yes, many new things happened to us at very last days of our stays there. Those days positioned us at the spot where we had to decide with no alternative because our next chance would not arrive anytime soon!) The first thing in the morning, Larry told me this *must* happen today or never. More than that, my husband informed me that if I won't be able to choose a partner, he will select the guy himself and will invite him to our room for a threesome he fantasized about. This warning worked. I picked the gentleman, and three of us had fun.

Thank you, Larry! That evening gave me an opportunity to make one of the most important discoveries on my Lifestyle journey. I cannot imagine our present sexual life without new friends belonging to various races. It would not be complete and fully thrilling without them.

Are people of different races dramatically unlike each other sexually? Yes, they are! If you were unable to find whatever you prefer in swingers of one race, you would find it in those belonging to the other one.

Here are my generalizations:
- Asian women have bodies of teenagers with small breasts and narrow buttocks.
- Even in a dark room, identifying a black female is easy because of her exceptionally soft and sensitive skin, not to mention all her exclusive body curves.
- Latin girls are feminine, with good deal of bottom parts, great curly hair, and dazzling eyes.

- No matter if they are of "giving" or "receiving" type, most white ladies are open-minded and ready to experiment with their sexuality. Many of them are bisexual.
- Black gentlemen sure do seem to have a bigger penis. They are energetic, long-lasting, and determined.
- White gentlemen, as a rule, are tender, calm, and love foreplay and oral sex, both giving and receiving.
- Most Asian gentlemen have a small frame and are seldom overweight. They look naturally groomed since they don't have much body hair. They are never initially over-aggressive but expect from their playmates a sufficient attention in return for delivered pleasure.
- Hispanic gentlemen are often inpatient, fast in their movements and have a higher-than-average stamina. Most of the time, long foreplay is not among their priorities.

Race-related disparities are not about external qualities and a person's looks only. The whole process of having sex with partners of different races is dissimilar as well.

Asian ladies' sexual culture is unique, which was a nice surprise for Larry. Before, his priorities were tall, slender women with long legs. However, his first Japanese playmate, who had nothing in common with the woman of his dream, instantly took him away. She concentrated on doing anything to deliver him maximum sexual pleasure. Yet she did not only have sex for him, she tremendously enjoyed her part too.

At one private party, I was chatting with a famous porn star, a black stud with an 11-inch souvenir. (Most porn stars are swingers, too.) I asked him what women he likes the most. His initial answer was, "All of you!" I insisted on details, and he confessed, "Asian ones are most exciting for me because my penis looks even larger in their small hands. And this thrills me a lot!"

Some swingers prefer their partners to be of certain races. It all depends on experiences and expectations. You would not spot these preferences at our profiles on the Web or at our ads, though. We only would reveal them in private. My girlfriend said to me once, "I don't care about my partners' color. Every color goes as long as it is black!" We both knew that was just a joke: swingers all have their likes and dislikes, but often those are just *preferences,* not requirements. Most Lifestylers are always open to new contacts and do not discriminate by race as well as by any other criteria. Genuine swingers are essentially EOP—Equal Opportunity Players!

Both of us, the authors of this book, like sushi and jerk chicken. Thanks to being in the Lifestyle, we now love Japanese girls and Jamaican guys. (As Larry just asked me to add, Jamaican girls are *something,* too!)

Get in the right mood!
By Larry and Mia

> *He said, don't keep me waitin' when I'm in the mood!*
> —Glenn Miller

You can begin a party even earlier than it starts and have an extra one or two hours of fun. This does not mean you have to come to the hosts' house or swing club any earlier.

As you know, the whole atmosphere at swing parties is not exactly ordinary and requires some time to adjust. Inexperienced people often get lost at the first stage of our get-togethers. Sometimes, they need considerable time to find their right behavior, hence to become a part of the fun.

Even if both of you are uninhibited and tension-free, even if you do not require any time at all switching from the vanilla demeanor to a swinging one, consider making your preparation *part of the event.* Establish your own pre-party routine (call it *ritual* if you wish) for you to get ready for action in advance and arrive fully warmed up and fully prepared. This way you would prolong your actual fun and receive additional satisfaction.

- Coordinate your preparation schedules. Agree on an exact time you both will be ready to leave. If something goes wrong (problem with makeup or hair or shoe decisions), let your partner know you are running late. Never make him/her nervous.
- Concentrate your thoughts on the event. Discuss the venue, recall people you know will be there and your experiences with them. Never talk negatively.
- Relax yourself with your favorite drink. A glass of good wine or champagne can release your mind from your usual bouquet of everyday worries and serve as the best helper for your makeup.
- Use special and unique visual, sound, and scent associations that could emotionally tune you up the right way. While getting ready to leave, we put porn on the TV on mute. We are not, *per se*, watching it, but a brief glance at the screen moves our mood in the right direction. We always listen to the music special to both of us since we only play a particular CD while we are getting ready for our Lifestyle evenings. Taking a shower, styling your hair, and applying a body lotion while listening to these sounds make us feel different compared with the same procedures done every morning while watching the news and listening weather forecasts before leaving for the office. We both use particular perfumes designated for our fun times only.
- Continue the music therapy in the car while you commute to the party place.

All this foreplay can help you toggle from an ordinary mindset to an exceptional one and help you reach that special internal mode of elevated emotional and physical expectations. As a result, you will be able to start enjoying the evening from its beginning, well before everyone else will.

Glossary

AC/DC—Bisexual.

All Cultures—All fetishes and sexual activities.

Analingus—Oral stimulation of the anus.

Arts—Fetishes.

Bareback play—Play without the use of condoms.

BBC—Big Black Cock.

BBW—Big Beautiful Woman.

B&D or BD—Bondage and Discipline.

BDSM—Bondage-Discipline–Sadomasochism.

Bi or Bisexual—One who enjoys sex with both men and women.

Bi-Curious—One who is either just interested in or has had limited bisexual experience.

Bi-Friendly—One who might not be interested, but has nothing against being the object of bi-sexual desires.

BYOB—Bring Your Own Bottle.

BYOC—Bring Your Own Condoms.

BYOT—Bring Your Own Towel.

Can Entertain—Someone who is willing to invite others to his/her place.

Can Travel—Someone willing to travel, generally beyond an hour's drive.

Clean—Diseases and Drugs Free.

Closed Swinging—Using separate rooms.

Culture—Euphemism for fetishes or sexual arts.

Couple—Two people (most often male and female) playing together.

CPL—Couple.

Cunnilingus—Oral stimulation of the vagina/clitoris.

DD-Free or DD-Clean—Diseases and Drugs Free.

Domestic Training—Submissive obedience to chores of both an intimate and humiliating nature.

DP—Double Penetration, simultaneous vaginal and anal.

DVP—Double Vaginal Penetration, vaginal stimulation involving two penises at the same time.

F—Female.

Fellation—Oral stimulation of the penis.

Fetish—Sexual stimulation via non-sexual acts or objects.

FMF—One man/two women threesome.

French (French Culture)—Oral-genital activities.

Full Swap—Sex with other couples that includes anything up to and including actual intercourse.

Gay—Homosexual, generally a male, not always, though.

GBM—Gay Black Male.

Greek (Greek Culture)—Anal intercourse.

GWM—Gay White Male.

Hedonist—One who lives for the pursuit of pleasure.

Heterosexual—Person who enjoys sex with only the opposite sex.

Homosexual—Person who enjoys sex with only the same sex.

Hung or **Well-hung**—One with a large penis.

HWP—Height/Weight Proportionate—Someone who is not overweight or underweight.

Indoor Sports—Swinging activities in general.

ISO—In Search Of.

Lesbian—Gay woman.

LMAO—Laughing my ass off.

LOL—Laughing Out Loud.

LTR—Long-term Relationship.

M—Male.

M&G—Meet-and-Greet.

MBC—Married Black Couple.

MBiC—Married Bi Couple.

Meet for Pleasure—Meet for swinging sex.

Ménage a Trois—Sexual encounter involving three people, a threesome.

MILF—Mother I'd Like (to) Fuck.

Moresome—More than four.

MWC—Married White Couple.

NBH—Nude Body (or Booby) Hug.

Off-Premise—Swing club or party where there are no designated locations for actual play.

On-Premise—Swing club/party where play area is equipped and actual play fully supported and encouraged.

Open swinging—Sexual activities in the same room.

PDA—Public Display of Affection.

PDP— Public Display of Porn.

PITA—Pain in the ass.

Roman (Roman Culture)—Group sex, parties, orgies, etc.

S&M or SM—Sadism/Masochism.

Safe—Someone who is not at risk for becoming or causing a pregnancy.

Safe Play—Play with the use of condoms only.

SBF—Single Black Female.

SBiF—Single Bi Female.

SBiM—Single Bi Male.

SBM—Single Black Male.

SGL—Single.

Sodomy—Anal sex, possibly forced.

Soft Swap—Sex with other couples that includes anything up to but not including actual intercourse.

STD—Sexually Transmitted Disease.

STR8 or STR—Straight, a heterosexual person.

Submissive—One who is passive and wishes to be dominated.

Swap—Partners exchange.

SWF—Single White Female.

SWM—Single White Male.

TAN—Tested Antibody Negative for HIV virus.

Transsexual—One who has undergone conversion from one gender to the other.

TV (Transvestite)—One who receives sexual gratification by wearing clothes identified with the opposite sex; not necessarily homosexual.

Use Back Door—Anal Sex.
V-Safe—Vasectomy safe.
Vasectomy—A surgical operation to sterilize a male.
Versatile—Bisexual.
Water Sport—Sexual stimulation involving urination.
XOXO—Hugs and Kisses.

Index

AC/DC 185
Acting the part 82
Age 27, 53, 67, 90
    When to start swinging 77
Aggresiveness 76
Analingus 185
Appearance (see Attractive, see Clothing, see Looks)
Approaching (see Meeting)
Arts (see Fetishes) 185
Attitude 75, 82
Attractive 73, 75, 139

Bareback play (see also Safe Play) 185
Bars (see M&G)
BBC 185
BBW 185
B&D or BD (see BDSM) 185
BDSM 25, 185
Behavior (see Acting the part)
Bi, Bi-Sexual 172, 185
Bi-Curious 185
Bi-Friendly 185
Burned 49
BYOB 108, 185
BYOC 185
BYOT 185

Can Entertain 185
Can Travel 185
Card, business 105
Certifications (see Validations)
Cheating 18
Clean 185
Closed swinging 185
Clothing 74, 140, 159, 162
    Resorts 165
Clubs 108, 109, 112
    Strategies 114
Conversation among swingers 79

Culture (see Fetishes) 185
Condoms (see Safe Play)
Contacting (see also Websites, Communicating) 105
Conventions 152
Couple 40, 45, 185
    Dating 51
    Meeting 55
Couple-to-couple play 24
Cost (see Swinging, Cost)
CPL 185
Cunnilingus 185

Dating (see Couple, Dating)
DD-Free (also DD-Clean) 185
Desire (a Lifestyle resort) 150
Discretion 38, 56, 80
Doing One for the Team 47
Domestic training 185
DP 185
DVP 186

Emails (see Websites, Communicating)
Erectile Dysfunction 119
Exhibitionism 22

F 186
Fake orgasm 49
Fakes 101
Fellation 186
Fetish 186
First meeting (see Couples, Dating)
Flakes 102
FMF 186
Foursomes 24
French (French Culture) 186
Friend
    Converting 61
    Horizontal 15, 56
    Vertical 15, 38, 61

Swinging from A to Z

Fuck (the term) 16
Full swap 23, 63, 186

Gangbangs 24
Gay 172, 186
GBM 186
Greek (Greek Culture) 186
Group sex 24, 168
GWM 186

Hedonism II 143
Hedonist 186
Heterosexual 186
Homosexual (see Gay) 186
Hosting private parties 126
Hotel 124
Hung (or Well-hung; see also Penis Size) 186
HWP 186

Indoor sports 186
Internet (see Websites)
Interracial sex (see Sex, Interracial)
Intimacy, problems with getting too close 57
ISO 186

Jamaica (see Hedonism II) 34
Jealousy 117

Kinsey Institute 16

Lesbian (see Gay) 186
Lifestyle (see Swinging)
LMAO 186
LOL 186
Looks (see also Attractive) 73
LoveVoodoo single men's guide to the Lifestyle 139
LTR 186

M 186
M&G 106 186
MBC 186

MBiC 186
Meet & Greets (see M&G)
Meeting (see also Websites, Telephoning, M&G, Conventions) 105, 114, 141, 154
Meet for pleasure 186
Ménage a Trois 186
MILF 186
Morality 31, 71
MWC 187

NBH 187
Nudity 39, 146

Off-Premise 109, 187
On-Premise 112, 187
Open relationships 18
Open swinging (see Swinging, Open) 187
Orgies 25, 50, 168

Parties
  Commercial 123
  Non-commercial 124
Private 121, 126
  Activities 131
  Cost 129
  Invitation 130
  M/F balance 133
PDA (or PDP) 187
Penis Size (see also Erectile dysfunction) 175
Phoning (see Telephoning)
Photographs (see Websites, Pictures)
PITA 187
Play 16
Polygamists 17
Price (see Swinging, Cost)
Privacy (see Discretion)
Profile on website (see Website, Profile)
Pubic hair 74, 139

Roman (Roman Culture) 187
Rules 20, 50, 52, 68, 130

S&M or SM (see BDSM) 187
Safe 187
Safe play 41, 187
Same room 64
SBF 187
SBiF 187
SBiM 187
SBM 187
Screening (see also Parties, Private) 169
Separate rooms 64
Sex (see also Penis Size, and see also Orgies)
   Amount thought about 16
   Interracial 178
   Preparing your mind 181
SGL 187
Sign language 52
Singles 107, 135
Sodomy 187
Soft Swap 23, 63, 187
Spanking 25
STD (see Safe Play) 187
STR8 or STR 187
Straight play 26
Submissive 187
Swap (see Swinging) 187
Swing Clubs (see Clubs)
Swinging 187
   Addictive 26
   Choosing 13, 32, 37, 46
   Cost 27
   Definition 15, 187
   Friends (see Friends)
   History 14, 15
   Open 187
   Varieties 21
   Who are swingers? 71
   Why swing 17, 19, 40
SWF 187
SWM 187

TAN 187
Team (see Doing One for the Team)
Telephoning 100, 105
Theme parties (see Parties, Private; see Hedonism II)
Clothing 162
Threesomes 23
Transsexual 187
Trust 19, 40, 51, 65
TV (Transvestite) 187

Use Back Door 188

Validations 89, 92, 103, 104
Vanilla 15, 31, 38
Voyeurism 22
V-Safe 188
Versatile 188

Water Sport 188
Websites (see also Validations) 87
   Author profile 95
   Communicating 99
   Pictures 91, 104, 140
   Profile 88, 92, 102

XOXO 188

Made in the USA
Lexington, KY
25 June 2015